# INSTRUMENT *of* PEACE

*Meditations on the Prayer of Saint Francis*

ALAN PATON
Author of the Bestseller
*Cry, the Beloved Country*

# INSTRUMENT *of* PEACE

*Meditations on the Prayer of Saint Francis*

WHITAKER
HOUSE

*Publisher's Note:* This new edition from Whitaker House is a revision of Alan Paton's *Instrument of Thy Peace,* published by The Seabury Press in 1982. It has been updated for modern readers. Revisions include the addition of chapter titles and American English spelling; in some cases, the author's Bible citations have been updated with modern translations. However, the author's original premises and message have been retained.



**INSTRUMENT OF PEACE**
**Meditations on the Prayer of Saint Francis**

Alan Stewart Paton Will Trust
Trustees: Iain Ewing and Gareth Collingwood
Contact number: +27 31 765 5937
admin@alanpatontrust.co.za

Back cover photo courtesy of Campbell Collections/Alan Paton Centre/
Gandhi-Luthuli Documentation Centre of the University of KwaZulu-Natal

ISBN: 979-8-88769-380-4 • eBook ISBN: 979-8-88769-381-1
Printed in the United States of America



Whitaker House • 1030 Hunt Valley Circle • New Kensington, PA 15068
www.whitakerhouse.com

Library of Congress Cataloging-in-Publication Data
Names: Paton, Alan, author.
Title: Instrument of peace : meditations on the prayer of Saint Francis / Alan Paton.
Description: New Kensington, PA : Whitaker House, [2025] | Summary: "Reflections on the Prayer of Saint Francis by the author of Cry, the Beloved Country, with the idea that those who contemplate the prayer, which begins, "Lord, make me an instrument of Thy peace," will come to the realization that God's love and peace are available despite dire circumstances"— Provided by publisher.
Identifiers: LCCN 2024056874 (print) | LCCN 2024056875 (ebook) | ISBN 9798887693804 (trade paperback) | ISBN 9798887693811 (ebook)
Subjects: LCSH: Prayer of St. Francis of Assisi—Meditations. | Catholic Church—Prayers and devotions. | Peace—Religious aspects—Catholic Church. | Spiritual life—Catholic Church.
Classification: LCC BV284.P73 P36 2025 (print) | LCC BV284.P73 (ebook) | DDC 242/.7—dc23/eng/20250117
LC record available at https://lccn.loc.gov/2024056874
LC ebook record available at https://lccn.loc.gov/2024056875



1 2 3 4 5 6 7 8 9 10 11 WH 32 31 30 29 28 27 26 25

# CONTENTS

# PREFACE

This book is written for sinners, and by one of them. It is written for those who wish with all their hearts to be better, purer, less selfish, more useful; for those who do not wish to be cold in love, and who know that being cold in love is perhaps the worst sin of them all; for those who wish to keep their faith bright and burning in a dark and faithless world; for those who seek not so much to lean on God as to be the active instruments of His peace.

I wrote also for those who are inclined to melancholy, for those who are inclined to withdraw rather than to participate, for those who are tempted to retreat into pietism because they are afraid of active engagement in the world, for those who deceive themselves that to be pious is to be more faithful to the gospel than to concern themselves with the building of a more just order of society.

I believe I shall be able to help some of them—not so much out of my own strength, which is not considerable, but out of the strength of one of the greatest, sweetest, and purest of the disciples,

St. Francis of Assisi, who in his turn drew his strength from his Divine Master.

More and more as time goes by, the memory of Francis of Assisi comes to be treasured by the whole Christian world. Christians disagree about many things, but they seldom, perhaps never, disagree about St. Francis. It is impossible for any Christian to hear or read or pray the immortal "Lord, make me an instrument of Thy peace," and not realize that he or she is in the presence of holiness.

It was nearly fifteen years ago that *Instrument of Thy Peace* was written. It was written during a time of great stress and anxiety. My wife Dorrie, to whom I had been married for thirty-nine years, was dying, slowly and painfully, of the terrible complaint known as emphysema.

Although the book is fifteen years old, it still speaks to me clearly. I can come to only one conclusion, that I was given help to write it. I can only relate the strange experience that as I reread it, there are parts of it that help and move me as though some other hand had written them.

Alan Paton
12 October 1981

# THE PRAYER OF SAINT FRANCIS

Lord, make me an instrument of Thy peace.
Where there is hatred, let me sow love;
Where there is injury, pardon;
Where there is doubt, faith;
Where there is despair, hope;
Where there is sadness, joy;
Where there is darkness, light.
O Divine Master, grant that I may not so much seek
To be consoled, as to console;
Not so much to be understood, as to understand,
Not so much to be loved, as to love.

For it is in giving that we receive,
It is in pardoning that we are pardoned,
It is in dying that we are born again to eternal life.

# 1

# AN INSTRUMENT OF THY PEACE

*Lord, make me an instrument of Thy peace.*
—Prayer of St. Francis

We pray for many things—for loved ones, for one sick, for one dying, for health, for much-needed money, for success in examinations, for our country, for the peace of the world. We pray for forgiveness of sins, for conquest of one particular sin that defeats us, for help in some situation that frightens or threatens us. We pray especially hard—most of us—when our own safety or security is threatened.

Sometimes we cannot pray because we are fallen into a melancholy, and therefore have for the time lost our hope and our faith and have no one to pray to.

I myself have done this, but now I wish to place on record that I am in unrepayable debt to Francis of Assisi, for when I pray his prayer, or even remember it, my melancholy is dispelled, my self-pity comes to an end, and my faith is restored because of this majestic conception of what the work of a disciple should be.

So majestic is this conception that one dare no longer be sorry for oneself. This world ceases to be one's enemy and becomes the place where one lives and works and serves. Life is no longer nasty, mean, brutish, and short, but becomes the time that one needs to make it less nasty and mean, not only for others, but indeed also for oneself.

We are brought back instantaneously to the reality of our faith, that we are not passive recipients but active instruments. The right relationship between man and God is instantly restored.

Francis of Assisi no doubt often prayed for something for himself, or for the order he had founded, or for the chapel and huts at Portiuncula, Italy. But in his prayer, he asks nothing for himself, or perhaps he asks everything, and that is that his whole life, all his gifts, his physical strength, shall be an instrument in God's hand.

And I say to myself, "This is the only way in which a Christian can encounter hatred, injury, despair, and sadness, and that is by throwing off his helplessness and allowing himself to be made the bearer of love, the pardoner, the bringer of hope, the comforter of those that grieve." And I believe that if you allow yourself to be so made, you will be so.

As I write this, I think of a man who is leaving prison to return to the world. During these years, he has paid more attention to religion than ever before in his life. As he leaves, the prison chaplain assures him that the past is done, the past is forgiven. But when he returns to the world, he finds that the world has not forgiven, that it has not forgiven his past. So hope changes to despair, faith to doubt. It seems that God has not forgiven him after all.

It is here that a great duty falls upon us all to be the bearers of God's forgiveness, to be the instrument of His love, to be active in compassion. This man's return to the world is made tragic because *we were not there*. God moves in His own mysterious ways, but a great deal of the time, He moves through us. And it is because we are not there that so many do not believe in God's love.

**Jesus:** *And He came to the disciples, and found them asleep, and said to Peter, What, could you not watch with Me one hour?* (Matthew 26:40)

**Jesus:** *You are the salt of the world. But if the salt should lose its taste, how can it be made salty again?* (Matthew 5:13 ISV)

**Dag Hammarskjöld**, former secretary-general of the United Nations, to himself on the eve of a meeting of the Security Council: Your responsibility is indeed terrifying. If you fail, it is God, thanks to you having betrayed Him, who will fail mankind. You fancy you can be responsible to God; can you carry the responsibility *for* God?

> O Lord, help us to be masters ourselves, that we may be servants for others.
>
> —**Sir Alexander Paterson,**
> who devoted his life and great talents to the reform of British prisons and institutions for delinquent boys and girls

## *PRAYER*

*O Lord, open my eyes that I may see the need of others, open my ears that I may hear their cries, open my heart so that they need not be without succor. Let me be not afraid to defend the weak because of the anger of the strong, nor afraid to defend the poor because of the anger of the rich. Show me where love and hope and faith are needed and use me to bring them to those places.*

*And so open my eyes and my ears that I may this coming day be able to do some work of peace for Thee.*

2

# NO ONE IS TOO WEAK

No one is too weak, too vile, too unimportant, to be God's instrument.

> *And Moses said to God, Who am I, that I should go to Pharaoh, and that I should bring forth the children of Israel out of Egypt? And He said, Certainly I will be with you; and this shall be a token to you, that I have sent you: When you have brought forth the people out of Egypt, you shall serve God upon this mountain.* (Exodus 3:11–12)

> *And Moses said to the* Lord, *O my Lord, I am not eloquent, neither heretofore, nor since You have spoken to Your servant: but I am slow of speech, and of a slow tongue. And the* Lord

> *said to him, Who has made man's mouth? or Who makes the dumb, or deaf, or the seeing, or the blind? have not I the* Lord*? Now therefore go, and I will be with your mouth, and teach you what you shall say.* (Exodus 4:10–12)

No Christian should ever think or say that he is not fit to be God's instrument, for that in fact is what it means to be a Christian. We may be humble about many things but may never decline to be used. John the Baptist told the people by the river Jordan, "I baptize you with water, for repentance, but the one who comes after me is mightier than I, and I am not fit to take off His shoes." (See Matthew 3:11.) Then Jesus Himself came to be baptized by him, and John tried to dissuade Him, saying to Him, "Do You come to me? I need rather to be baptized by You." Jesus replied, *"Allow it to be so now: for thus it becomes us to fulfill all righteousness"* (Matthew 3:15). So John baptized Him whose shoes he was not fit to take off.

The gospel is full of reassurances to us, some of them startling. You are salt to the world! You are light to all the world! Even the hairs of your head have all been counted! These words were exciting to those who heard them. Things might be dark, but they were to be the light of the world. They were given a new sense of their value as persons. Especially was this true of women. One can hardly describe the joy of the first disciples, for Jesus gave them such a sense of their significance in the world. This same sense of significance has been given again and again to other people by disciples of Jesus. Of those none was greater than Francis of Assisi. He might well have prayed:

> To those who have lost their way, let me restore it to them.
>
> To those who are aimless, let me bring purpose.
>
> To those who do not know who they are, let me teach them that they are the children of God and can be used as

His instruments in the never-ending work of healing and redemption.

There are therefore two things for us to do. The first is never to doubt that God can use us if we are willing to be used, no matter what our weaknesses. The second is to see that God can use any other person who is willing to be used, whatever his weaknesses, and if need be, to assure him of this truth.

## *THE LITTLE FLOWERS OF ST. FRANCIS OF ASSISI*[1]

One day as St. Francis was returning from his prayers in the wood, Brother Masseo met him. Wishing to test how humble he was, he asked in a mocking manner, "Why after thee? Why after thee? Why after thee?" St. Francis replied, "What is it thou wouldst say?" And Brother Masseo answered, "Say, why is it that all the world comes after thee, and everybody desires to see thee, and to hear thee, and to obey thee? Thou art not a man either comely of person, or of noble birth, or of great knowledge; whence then comes it that all the world runs after thee?"

Hearing this, St. Francis, filled with joy in his spirit, raised his face toward heaven and remained for a great while with his mind lifted up to God. Then returning to himself, he knelt down and gave praise and thanks to God. And then, with great fervor of spirit, turning to Brother Masseo, he said, "Wouldst know why after me? Wouldst know why after me? Why all the world

1. *The Little Flowers of St. Francis* (in Italian, *Fioretti di San Francesco*) is *florilegium* or excerpts from a collection on the life of Saint Francis of Assisi. Originally attributed to an anonymous author, most scholars now agree that it was composed by Ugolino Brunforte (1262–1348), an Italian Friar Minor.

follows after me? This comes to me because the eyes of the Most High God, which behold in all places both the evil and the good, even those most holy eyes have not seen amongst sinners one more vile, nor more insufficient, nor a greater sinner than I, and therefore to do that wonderful work which He intends to do, He hath not found on earth a viler creature than I; and for this cause, He elected me to confound the nobility, and the grandeur, and the strength, and beauty, and wisdom of the world, that all men may know that all virtue and all goodness are of Him, and not of the creature, and that none should glory in his presence, but that he who glories should glory in the Lord, to whom is all honor and glory in eternity!"

Then Brother Masseo, at this humble and fervent reply, feared within himself and knew certainly that St. Francis was grounded in humility.

## *PRAYER*

*Lord, make me willing to be used by Thee. May my knowledge of my unworthiness never make me resist being used by Thee. May I always remember the need of others so that I may ever be willing to be used by Thee.*

*And open my eyes and my heart that I may this coming day be able to do some work of peace for Thee.*

3

# LET ME SOW LOVE

*Where there is hatred, let me sow love.*
—Prayer of St. Francis

Let us leave aside for the time being the immensely difficult question of what we are to do when we ourselves hate, when we ourselves are the object of hatred, and the immensely difficult question of how one can possibly love one's enemies. Let us also leave aside for the time the immensely difficult question of how we can possibly love those who are cruel or unjust or indifferent to others. Our Lord enjoined us to love our enemies, but one of the harshest judgments He ever passed was on the man who would cause a child to stumble.

The petition of St. Francis may be taken for the moment in an easier way, namely that he asks to be the reconciler of those who hate one another, or that he asks to be able to soften the heart of one who hates and to heal the grief and resentment and lostness of one who is hated. This is something that we can ask for ourselves. We can plead with those who hate and encourage those who are hated; we can mediate between those who hate one another.

Yet this problem also will confront us with a great difficulty. A person who hates may find a transcendental reason (such as the love of Christ) why he should stop hating, and this becomes more important for him than his reasons for hating. This, of course, means that he undergoes a spiritual transformation, a conversion. But what of those who do not? How are we to help them? How are we to help people to find it easier not to hate?

Anglican Archbishop William Temple wrote:

> More potent than school or even than home, as a moral influence, is the whole structure of society and especially its economic structure. This fixes for all their place in the general scheme; and the way in which they gain and keep that place of necessity determines a great deal of their conduct and profoundly influences their outlook upon life.

To be the instrument of God's peace is not to confine oneself to the field of personal relationships, but to concern oneself also with the problems of human society—hunger, poverty, injustice, cruelty, exploitation, and war.

Some Christians argue that if we would only change men, then society itself would change. That there is some truth in this, none of us doubts. But the full truth is that we must try both to change man and to change society. There are some changes in man that cannot be achieved without some changes in society. The front is wider than that of pure evangelism.

Such a view arouses opposition, anger, and even hatred among anti-change Christians. They call it the *social gospel* and regard it as an adulteration of the teaching of Christ. We shall have to deal later with this opposition, this anger, and even this hatred.

## *THE LITTLE FLOWERS OF ST. FRANCIS OF ASSISI*

It came to the ears of Francis that a bitter quarrel had arisen between the bishop of Assisi and the city magistrates, and that bickering and anger were disfiguring the public life. Therefore Francis sent a message to the magistrates, asking them to go at once to the bishop's palace. Although they had all been excommunicated by the bishop, they agreed out of veneration for Francis. Meanwhile Francis went to the palace, and as soon as the magistrates appeared, he and his brothers began to sing the "Canticle of the Sun." Hearing the singing, the bishop came down to see what it was about, and as he came out of the door of the palace, the magistrates came in at the gate, and each eyed the other coldly.

Just as this happened, the brothers came to the new stanza that Francis had written for just this moment:

> Praised be my Lord for those who for Thy love forgive
> And weakness bear and tribulation
> Blessed those who shall in peace endure,
> For by Thee, most High, shall they be crowned.

Both bishop and magistrates were humbled by these words, and when the canticle was done, they advanced to meet each other and were reconciled.

**Bishop Brooke Foss Westcott:** Behold, O Lord God, our strivings after a truer and more abiding order. Give us visions that bring back a lost glory to the earth, and dreams that foreshadow the better order which Thou hast prepared for us. Scatter every excuse of frailty and unworthiness; consecrate us all with a heavenly mission: open to us a clear prospect of our work. Give us strength according to our day, gladly to welcome and gratefully to fulfill it, through Jesus Christ our Lord.

## *PRAYER*

*Take all hate from my heart, O God, and teach me how to take it from the hearts of others. Open my eyes and show me what things in our society make it easy for hatred to flourish and hard for us to conquer it. Then help me to try to change these things.*

*And so open my eyes and my ears that I may this coming day be able to do some work of peace for You.*

# 4

# BORN OF GOD

*Every one that loves is born of God, and knows God. He that loves not knows not God; for God is love.*
—1 John 4:7–8

This is a tremendous saying, and it carries a most tremendous message to those who are faithful yet at times are troubled by doubt, to those who are doubtful yet at times are troubled by faith. It carries this tremendous message to those who already love Christ, but who are terrified and appalled and bewildered by the great superstructure of the beliefs and the theologies and the ordinances and the disunities and the irrelevancies of Christianity and the churches. I shall not easily forget reading Malcolm Muggeridge on the crucifixion in the 1967 Easter Sunday issue of *The Observer.* Mr. Muggeridge writes that he "can grasp some sort of notion of a Deity, and of his loving purpose, in which I, in common with all creation, am inextricably enmeshed." But he cannot believe in the virgin birth, or that Jesus was God's Son "in any particular sense," or in the resurrection.

Muggeridge writes:

> I even prefer to suppose that some body-snatcher, accustomed to hang about Golgotha to pick up anything that might be going, heard in his dimwitted way that the King of the Jews was up for execution. Good! he thinks; there are bound to be pickings there. So he waits till the job is done, finds out where the corpse has been laid, drags the stones away, and then, making sure no one is watching, decamps with the body.
>
> What a disappointment for him! This King of the Jews has no crown, no jewels, no orbs, no sceptre, no ring; he is just a worthless, wasted, broken, naked body. The man contemptuously abandons the body to the vultures, who in their turn leave the bones to whiten in the sun.
>
> Those precious, precious bones!

And I say to myself, what does one say to any person who wants to believe and who cannot believe ... or who certainly cannot believe it all? What does one say to one who loves Christ and cannot believe in the virgin birth or the resurrection? What does one say to one who wants to believe that God is the kind of God that Jesus believed Him to be, one who wants to worship Him, but cannot accept the accumulation of creeds and articles and doctrines that seem in the eyes of the churches to be inseparable from God? What does one say to one who writes with such longing disbelief of "those precious, precious bones," yet believes them to be only the bones of an ordinary man?

This problem is a real one. Was this wonderful man wonderful only when he taught morality and not when he taught theology? Was his knowledge sound about man and unsound about the divine and the supernatural? Was his life magnificent but was he unsound on sex and marriage and divorce?

I myself no longer presume to answer these questions with assurance. I cannot construct a body of belief that will be acceptable to all. The Protestant theologian Leslie Weatherhead, whose integrity I would never question, rejects miracle after miracle, and doctrine after doctrine, and then says he believes in the resurrection.

Is there nothing to hold on to? I believe there is, and it is that God is love, that if I love, I am a child of God, and if I am unloving, I know not God. So I would say to those who love Christ and want to follow Him but are afraid of the doctrines and the theology, that they respond in all confidence to the call, "Take heart, it is I, do not be afraid." (See Matthew 14:27.)

He came and took me by the hand
Up to a red rose tree,
He kept His meaning to Himself
But gave a rose to me.
I did not pray Him to lay bare
The mystery to me,
Enough the rose was Heaven to smell
And His own face to see.

**—Ralph Hodgson**

**Lancelot Andrewes**, the English bishop: O Lord, perfect for me that which is lacking of Thy gifts: of faith, increase my littleness of faith; of hope, establish trembling hope; of love, kindle its smoking flame; shed abroad Thy love in my heart, withal to love

Thee, my friend in Thee, mine enemy for Thee. Let me fear one thing only, the fearing aught more than Thee.

## *PRAYER*

> *O God, Creator of mankind, I do not aspire to comprehend You or Your creation, nor to understand pain or suffering. I aspire only to relieve the pain and suffering of others, and I trust that in doing so, I may understand more clearly Your nature—that You are the Father of all mankind, and that the hairs of my head are numbered.*
>
> *And help me this coming day to do some work of peace for You.*

# 5

# LET ME SOW FAITH

*Where there is doubt, let me sow faith.*
—Prayer of St. Francis

Here, St. Francis is not referring to that kind of doubt that accompanies the search for truth. He refers to doubt of God's love and goodness, which was one of the great themes of the teaching of Jesus.

> *And when he came to His disciples, he saw a great multitude about them, and the scribes questioning with them. And immediately all the people, when they beheld him, were greatly amazed, and running to Him saluted Him. And he asked the scribes, What question you with them? And one of the multitude answered and said, Master, I have brought to You my son, which has a dumb spirit; and wherever he takes him, he*

> *tears him: and he foams, and gnashes with his teeth, and pines away: and I spoke to your disciples that they should cast him out; and they could not. He answered him, and said, O faithless generation, how long shall I be with you? how long shall I suffer you? bring him to Me. And they brought him to Him: and when He saw him, immediately the spirit tore him; and he fell on the ground, and wallowed foaming. And He asked his father, How long is it ago since this came to him? And he said, Of a child. And often it has cast him into the fire, and into the waters, to destroy him: but if You can do any thing, have compassion on us, and help us. Jesus said to him, If you can believe, all things are possible to him that believes. And immediately the father of the child cried out, and said with tears, Lord, I believe; help You my unbelief.* (Mark 9:14–24)

I believe—help my unbelief! That indeed is the cry of many of us, for our faith is many times put to the test, by the failure of our ideals to triumph, by the long illness of some beloved person, by world disasters, by wars and rumors of wars. "Why does God allow it?" is a question one often hears. "Is God really a loving God when He permits such things to happen?" "Can God really be all-powerful? For if He is all-powerful, then He cannot be loving."

Sometimes these questions are asked by people who want to rid themselves of the belief in God, but sometimes they are asked by people who want to keep their faith in God and who hope for reassuring answers to these disturbing questions.

As far as we know, Francis of Assisi never asked himself these questions. If there was sorrow, he asked to be allowed to bring joy. If there was darkness, he asked to be allowed to bring light. If there was grief, he asked to be allowed to bring comfort. This concept of discipleship was sublime. If the creation groaned and travailed until now (see Romans 8:22), then he would not question but would devote himself to the relieving of its pain and the assuaging of its grief.

There is even more to it than this, for in taking upon himself the sorrow of the world, as his own Master had done before him, St. Francis was a living witness to the activity of God's love in the world. God's love, though it is not limited to us as instruments, nevertheless uses us as instruments, so that those who are in need of it find it in us. It is possible that some will never find it if they do not find it in us. And it is also possible that some will not believe in it, because they do not find it in us. "If *you* are a follower of Christ," they say, "I want no part of Him."

So the matters of faith and of love are seen to be inseparable. If we do not love, then others will not have faith.

> *Philip said to Him, Lord, show us the Father, and it suffices us. Jesus said to him, Have I been so long time with you, and yet have you not known Me, Philip? he that has seen Me has seen the Father; and how say you then, Show us the Father? Believe you not that I am in the Father, and the Father in Me? the words that I speak to you I speak not of Myself: but the Father that dwells in Me, He does the works.*
>
> (John 14:8–10)

> *A new commandment I give to you, That you love one another; as I have loved you, that you also love one another. By this shall all men know that you are My disciples, if you have love one to another.* (John 13:34–35)

## *PRAYER*

> *Help me, O lord, to be more loving. Help me, O Lord, not to be afraid to love the outcast, the leper, the unmarried pregnant*

*woman, the traitor to the state, the man out of prison. Help me by my love to restore the faith of the disillusioned, the disappointed, the early bereaved. Help me by my love to be the witness of Thy love.*

*And may I this coming day be able to do some work of peace for Thee.*

# 6

# FORGIVE US OUR TRESPASSES

*Forgive us our trespasses,*
*as we forgive those who trespass against us.*
—Jesus (the Lord's Prayer in the Book of Common Prayer)

*Repent you: for the kingdom of heaven is at hand.*
—John the Baptist (Matthew 3:2)

*The fully forgiven man does not rejoice in his own forgiveness*
*but in the divine love to which he owes it;*
*and his past sin persists in his experience no longer as a*
*source of shame but as the occasion of a new wonder in his*
*adoration of the love divine.*
—William Temple

He who is able to love himself is able to love others also; he who has learned to overcome self-contempt has overcome his contempt for others. —Paul Tillich

It is in pardoning that we are pardoned.

**—St. Francis**

It was thirty years ago at a penal reform congress in Johannesburg that I first encountered the extraordinary theological view that when a man commits an offense, he rends the moral order of the universe, and that this damage is repaired only by his punishment. This extraordinary theology underlay much of our penal practice in South African courts and prisons at that time.

This theory was discarded in respect of juvenile offenders in 1934, and later in respect of adult first offenders, but it still prevails in our ordinary prisons, though even there, a system of gradual relaxation of restrictions is applied.

The sequence "offense, punishment" was once considered complete. The punishment cancelled out the offense in some mysterious way, even when, for the rest of his life, the offender had to declare his offense on certain official documents, such as an application for a passport. Even more baffling was the question of what happened to the moral order of the universe when the offender was never caught.

The Christian sequence is quite different. It runs "offense, forgiveness, restoration." It is doubtful even whether repentance is an essential term in the sequence. In the story of the woman taken in adultery, Jesus says to her, "*Neither do I condemn you: go, and sin no more*" (John 8:11), but whether she repented or not, we do not know. In His injunction that we should love our enemies and pray for them that despitefully use us, there is no mention of their repentance. (See Matthew 5:44.) In fact, the implication is that they do not repent. *We must therefore learn to forgive unconditionally.* We must even eschew the use of that fascinating statement, "I forgive but I do not forget."

The sequence is, however, quite different when we ourselves are the offenders. Whether God requires repentance before He forgives, I do not presume to know. But I presume to know that for us ourselves, repentance is essential before we can feel forgiven, and this also seems to be the belief of the church.

I should like to write a few words for those who *have* repented and who *have* been forgiven—whether in private or public confession, or by the person whom they have harmed—but who still *cannot feel forgiven.*

There is something wrong with you. You are literally not understanding the gospel. You are not understanding the injunction of Jesus to you that you must not forgive your brother seven times, but *"seventy times seven"* (Matthew 18:22). For if you are expected to do that, what do you think God may be expected to do? What is more, you are making it difficult, if not impossible, for God to use you as an instrument because of your feeling of guilt for something that has been forgiven.

Paul Tillich, in his great sermon "You Are Accepted," says what we have to do is simply to accept the fact that we are accepted. *"Beloved, now are we the sons of God, and it does not yet appear what we shall be"* (1 John 3:2). Tillich says, "But sometimes it happens that we receive the power to say 'Yes' to ourselves, that peace enters into us and makes us whole, that self-hate and self-contempt disappear and that our self is reunited with itself. Then we say that grace has come upon us."

There is a well-known saying, "I am at peace with the world," but it is much more important to be able to say, "I am at peace with myself." In the poem "Desiderata," by Max Ehrmann, there is the wise admonition: "Beyond a wholesome discipline, be gentle with yourself."

> For many men and women believe that God is All-Mighty and may do all; and that He is All-Wisdom and can do all; but that He is All-Love and will do all—there they stop short.
>
> And it is this lack of knowing that most hinders God's lovers. For when they begin to hate sin, and to amend them by the ordinance of Holy Church, yet there dwells a dread that stirs them to beholding of themselves and of their sins before done. And this dread they take for a meekness; but this is a foul blindness, and a weakness if we cannot despise it. For if we knew it that, we should suddenly despise it, as we do another sin that we know; for it comes of the enemy, and it is against the truth.
>
> For of all the properties of the blessed Trinity, it is God's will that we have most sureness in liking and love. For Love makes Might and Wisdom full meek to us. For right as by the courtesy of God He forgets our sins when we repent, right so will He that we forget our sin, and all our heaviness, and all our doubtful dreads.
>
> **—Lady Julian of Norwich,**
> **in *Revelations of Divine Love***

**Frederick MacNutt:** O Lord, forgive what I have been, sanctify what I am, and order what I shall be.

***Book of Common Prayer*:** We acknowledge and bewail our manifold sins and wickedness, which we, from time to time, most grievously have committed, by thought, word, and deed, against Thy Divine Majesty....

***Book of Common Prayer***: Almighty God ... have mercy upon you; pardon and deliver you from all your sins; confirm and strengthen you in all goodness; and bring you to everlasting life; through Jesus Christ our Lord.

## *PRAYER*

*Lord, let no unnecessary sense of guilt prevent me from being used by Thee. Let not the knowledge of my unworthiness prevent me from being used by Thee. Lord, never let the forgiven past prevent me from being used by Thee.*

*And may I this coming day be able to do some work of peace for Thee.*

# 7

# LET ME BRING HOPE

*Where there is despair, let me bring hope.*
—Prayer of St. Francis

There is no more terrible condition of the soul than despair. In a way, it brings life to an end, yet we continue to breathe, to eat, and to drink. But we hope no more.

When we despair, most of us cannot turn our faces to the wall and die. Even our despair does not destroy our sense of duty, except in extreme cases. If we have dependents, we must continue to work. But in the old monasteries, those who did not perform work were in danger of lapsing into sloth, often called *accidie* or *acedia*. This is not an extreme form of laziness as some suppose but the dark night of the soul. There is nothing to live for, fight for, pray for. In earlier days, it was counted one of the seven deadly sins, and although we have today a fuller understanding of it, it is important to note that even in despair, we are not absolved from responsibility, not only for others, but for ourselves.

Sometimes an external event brings on despair. The work of a lifetime may be destroyed in a moment. An outbreak of war destroys the lifelong work of a man for peace. A cyclone ruins in a few moments a man's farm, destroys his house, kills his cattle, lays waste his crops, takes away his soil.

Sometimes the external event is so terrible that hardly one of us would not despair. But sometimes the external event is not visible to others. Some people fall into a despair over the irredeemable wickedness of man, whereas we know that man is not irredeemably wicked. It would seem that in most cases of despair, there is also in us a predisposition to despair. Some escape despair by way of cynicism, but one imagines that St. Francis would have prayed for cynics also.

And here it should be recorded that St. Francis himself passed through a period of despair lasting two years. One of his biographers, Father Isidore O'Brien, attributed this to the fear that his rule of poverty would be modified, to his disillusionment over the gross behavior of many of the Crusaders, and to his increasing physical blindness. Yet clearly there was something deeply wrong in himself. He withdrew from the world, he who had asked to be the instrument of God's peace. He visited no more the convent of the Poor Clares, lest it should be a source of scandal. It was Clare herself who used all her holiness and skill to restore him to himself. She appealed to him to visit them and not forsake them. The visit was a failure. He did not preach to them as was his custom. Instead, he sprinkled ashes upon his head and recited the psalm, *Miserere mei, Deus—"Have mercy upon me, O God"* (Psalm 51:1). Then he left them.

But Clare would not accept defeat. In Father O'Brien's significant words, she saw that "Francis needed human help to draw him out of himself." She next asked to be allowed to dine with the brothers at Portiuncula, and so great was her insistence that Francis could not deny her.

## *THE LITTLE FLOWERS OF ST. FRANCIS OF ASSISI*

When Clare arrived at the Portiuncula, she went into the chapel of St. Mary of the Angels and devoutly saluted the Virgin Mary, before whose altar her hair had been cut off when she received the veil. Meanwhile Francis set out the meal on the bare ground, as was his custom. Then he and one of the brothers, and Clare and the sister who had accompanied her, sat down together, surrounded by the rest of the brothers, sitting humbly around them. When the fish dish was served, Francis began to speak of God so sweetly, so sublimely, and in a manner so wonderful, that the grace of God fell upon them all, and all were rapt in Christ.

Now the people of Assisi and Bettona and of all the country around about saw St. Mary of the Angels as it were on fire, with the convent and the woods adjoining. The people of Assisi hastened with great speed to put out the fire, but upon arriving, they saw no fire, only Francis and Clare and all their companions sitting around their humble meal on the ground. Then they knew that what they had seen was a celestial fire.

It was not only Clare who helped Francis out of his despair, nor did his despair end merely because Pope Honorius III approved his amended rule of poverty. He heard Christ, by way of rebuke, say to him (and some of us):

"Why art thou distressed? Have I so set thee a shepherd over My religion that thou knowest not I am its chief Protector? I set thee over it, a simple man, to the end that those who will, may follow thee in those things I work in thee for an example to others. It is I who have called them; I who will keep and feed them; and I will make good the falling away of some by putting others in their place, in such wise that if these others be not born, I will cause them to be born."

What part Francis himself played in his own liberation, it is hard to determine. But many writers on despair believe that the person in despair must help to liberate himself. He can be helped by others by the grace of God, but his own action is required.

Anglican priest and poet John Keble advised, "When you find yourself overpowered as it were by melancholy, the best way is to go out and do something kind to somebody or other."

In *The Way of Silence,*[2] mystic teacher Adela M. Curtis wrote:

> If you have a negative feeling (worry, fear, anxiety, hate, resentment) and it does not go away when you meditate, you must take immediate action. ... Instead of sitting down in front of that mood to wrestle with it by denials, *do* an heroic thing ... make yourself act quickly on the opposite side of that state. ... You have no idea of the virtue of acting on what you know is right if you want to overcome your feelings or nerves. There is some fear in it too. It ought to appeal to your sporting instincts.

---

2. Adela M. Curtis, *The Way of Silence (Studies in Meditation),* (London: School of Meditation, 1933).

What simple advice to relieve the darkest illness of the soul! And I believe it is right. I give my own testimony that when I am tempted to despair, when I am tempted to believe in the futility of all endeavor, when I believe that the love of God is not actively helping me, I pray or speak or read this prayer of St. Francis, which is the subject of these meditations, and I decide to act on it, or I should rather say, *I am moved to act on it.* From that moment, the temptation to despair is ended. Therefore I am in this unrepayable debt.

When his life's work was threatened, St. Ignatius of Loyola was asked what he would do if Pope Paul IV dissolved or otherwise acted against the Society of Jesus, to which Ignatius had devoted his energy and gifts. He replied, "I would pray for fifteen minutes, then I would not think of it again."

## *PRAYER*

*Lord, save me from despair, and if I am in despair, make me to do some work of peace for Thee.*

# 8

# CONSIDER THE LILIES OF THE FIELD

*Therefore I say to you, Take no thought for your life, what you shall eat, or what you shall drink; nor yet for your body, what you shall put on. Is not the life more than meat, and the body than raiment? Behold the fowls of the air: for they sow not, neither do they reap, nor gather into barns; yet your heavenly Father feeds them. Are you not much better than they? Which of you by taking thought can add one cubit to his stature? And why take you thought for raiment? Consider the lilies of the field, how they grow; they toil not, neither do they spin: and yet I say to you, That even Solomon in all his glory was not arrayed like one of these.*

—Matthew 6:25–29

This is not one of the easiest passages in the Gospels. Nor am I necessarily a suitable person to write about these particular anxieties because I do not have them. I have known men sacked, fired from their jobs in middle age, at that very time of life when it is hard for a man to get another. Our own duty in such cases is plain, and that is to show friendship and give what help will be accepted. But what else can we say to the anxious man? Can we say to him that he is worth more than the birds, when we know that more people suffer today from hunger and poverty than ever before in the history of man?

Can we say to the parents of teenagers in this modern world that they should not be anxious? Can we say to the parents of a son or daughter who is travelling in a plane that has gone silent over the sea or the mountains that they should not be anxious? Of course we cannot. There is only one thing that one can do in such cases of anxiety and that is to pray for one's friends and show one's friendship toward them.

(I have a friend who has said to me, on more than one occasion, "You must not worry. I *know* everything will be all right." I think his statement is absurd, and I could not make it myself to another. But I know he is trying to comfort me, and I love him for that. I think on the whole I would prefer him to a friend who said, "You must hope for the best, but you must prepare for the worst." However, I don't really know. I think it would depend on the way my friends said it!)

I do not think Jesus is teaching us about particular cases of anxiety. I think He is teaching us not to be *anxious persons*. And He strongly suggests in this passage that this anxiousness in us is caused because our scale of values is wrong. I have a friend, a good woman, a faithful churchwoman, who is perpetually anxious; yet her life has been characterized by what appears to me to be continuous happiness. She appears to me to be not thankful enough for what *has happened* to her and instead to be overanxious about what *might happen* to her.

We ourselves who are not anxious persons can well act in the spirit of Francis, which is the spirit of Christ, toward those who are. Our duty is clear. And those who are overanxious must face the truth that their faith in the God whom Jesus taught, who is indeed our Father, is not adequate, and that there is no point in believing in the Christian God at all if we do not believe that we are in His care. And they must also face the truth that if they are overanxious, they cannot be of much help to others.

## *A TALE THAT I KNEW IN MY CHILDHOOD*

The inn was full, and the innkeeper sent the maid down to the cellar to draw more ale. When after much time she had not appeared, the innkeeper went down to the cellar to see what had happened to her. There she was sitting, weeping before the cask, while the ale was running to waste. The innkeeper quickly closed the tap and said angrily to her, "What is this all about?"

With tearful eyes she pointed to the beam above the cask, on which was lying a hammer.

"I was thinking, master," she said, "one day my little daughter may be working at the inn, and she may be sent down here to draw the ale, and the hammer may fall on her head and kill her."

**John Bunyan,** *The Pilgrim's Progress*: Looking very narrowly before him as he went, he espied two lions in the way. Now, thought he, I see the dangers that Mistrust and Timorous were driven back by. ... Then he was afraid, and thought also himself to go back after them, for he thought nothing but death was before him. But the Porter at the lodge, whose name is Watchful, perceiving that Christian made a halt as if he would go back, cried unto him saying, "Is thy strength so small? Fear not the lions, for they are chained, and are placed there for trial of faith where it is, and for discovery of those that have none: keep in the midst of the path, and no hurt shall come unto thee."

However, one cannot make light of deep and persistent anxiety. Dr. James Reid tells of a man who suffered from periodic attacks of acute anxiety that prayer did not seem to help. In one of his dark moments, the man went to a friend, who advised him to commit himself to God, even if he had to accept his recurrent fear as a wounded soldier accepts his disability. The result, writes Dr. Reid, was gradual, but in the end, there was a total release.

To commit oneself to God is to make oneself an instrument of His peace. In acting for Him, we do not have so much time to worry about ourselves. In the end, we may cease to worry about ourselves altogether.

Jesus gave advice to people who are too anxious:

> *First be concerned about God's kingdom and his righteousness, and all of these things will be provided for you as well. So never worry about tomorrow, because tomorrow will worry about itself. Each day has enough trouble of its own.*
>
> (Matthew 6:33–34 ISV)

*Let not your heart be troubled: you believe in God, believe also in Me.* (John 14:1)

## *PRAYER*

*O Lord, save us from anxiety, and if we are anxious, let us commit ourselves to You more fully, to be used as the instruments of Your peace, so that we learn to be less concerned about ourselves and more concerned about others.*

*And may we this coming day be able to do some work of peace for You.*

# 9

# YOUR WILL BE DONE

*And He came out, and went, as He was wont, to the mount of Olives; and His disciples also followed Him. And when He was at the place, He said to them, Pray that you enter not into temptation. And He was withdrawn from them about a stone's cast, and kneeled down, and prayed, saying, Father, if You be willing, remove this cup from Me: nevertheless not My will, but Yours, be done. And there appeared an angel to Him from heaven, strengthening Him. And being in an agony He prayed more earnestly: and His sweat was as it were great drops of blood falling down to the ground. And when He rose up from prayer, and was come to His disciples, He found them sleeping for sorrow, and said to them, Why sleep you? rise and pray, lest you enter into temptation.*

—Luke 22:39–46

This is one of the most wonderful passages in the Gospels because it shows that Jesus was not God pretending to be a man. In the garden of Gethsemane, Jesus told Peter, James, and John that his soul was *"exceeding sorrowful, even to death"* (Matthew 26:38), which another translation renders as *"my heart is ready to break with grief"* (NEB). Mark 14:33 (ISV) says Jesus was *"distressed and troubled."* The *New English Bible* translates this verse as, *"Horror and dismay came over him"* (NEB). According to St. Luke, Jesus asked that if it were God's will, He should be spared the cross. According to St. Matthew, He asked to be spared "if it is possible." According to the first three Gospels, He concluded His petition with the words, *"Your will be done,"* or more strongly, *"Nevertheless not My will, but Yours, be done"* (Luke 22:42).

What was happening there in Gethsemane? I am not a theologian or a learned scholar, but it seems plain to me that Jesus was filled with fear of His impending death; it was the first time in His life, so far as we know, that He had been afraid. A short time before this, He had told His disciples not to let their hearts be troubled, yet now His own heart was ready to break with grief. More than once, He had told His disciples that He must die; now He asked God not to let Him die.

The story is not finished yet. He suddenly rises from the ground and goes to His sleeping disciples and says to them, *"The hour has come"* (Matthew 26:45 NEB). When Judas comes with the soldiers, He does not resist. He says, "Let the Scriptures be fulfilled." To the man who strikes at the high priest's servant, He says, *"Put up your sword. All who take the sword shall die by the sword"* (Matthew 26:52 NEB). He then says those strange words, *"Do you suppose that I cannot appeal to my Father, who would at once send to my aid more than twelve legions of angels?"* (Matthew 26:53–54 NEB). But He adds that this cannot be.

To me as a writer, this is an unsurpassable picture of a man struggling with God and with destiny, all in the framework of a great obedience. So do we all struggle, and though not always with the same obedience, we wish it might be so.

During the trial, the struggle seems to have ceased for a while. Indeed, after the trial, on the Via Dolorosa, He turns to the women mourning and lamenting and says, *"Weep not for Me, but weep for yourselves, and for your children"* (Luke 23:28). In the physical agony of the cross, He remembered His mother (see John 19:26–27), but in the spiritual agony that accompanies it, He utters that loud and desolate cry, *"Eli, Eli, lama sabachthani?"* which is interpreted, *"My God, My God, why have You forsaken Me?"* (Matthew 27:46; Mark 15:34).

This story is not finished yet. According to St. John, He again cried out aloud, and this time He says, *"It is finished"* (John 19:30). And according to St. Luke, He gives up His life with the words, *"Father, into Your hands I commend My spirit"* (Luke 23:46).

So there it all is, an agony of grief and fear, a rousing of one-self to face the ultimate ordeal, an act of peace to repair an act of violence, a remembrance under sentence of death of the women of Jerusalem and of his mother, one cry of utter desolation, and another that the work is finished, a commending of Himself into the hands of God.

No wonder that Francis of Assisi so loved this Man and followed Him as his Lord and Brother. For if there has to be grief, if there has to be fear, if there has to be desolation, let there also be a continuous remembrance of others, a finishing, a commending of one's spirit into the hands of God. For the first is a wound, and the second is a healing. The first is a judgment on life, the second is a vindication. The first is a curse, the second is a benediction. Even so, Lord, may it be with us.

## *THE LITTLE FLOWERS OF ST. FRANCIS OF ASSISI*

*The Leper on the Umbrian Plain:* One day, Francis was riding on the Umbrian Plain, on his way home to Assisi. Though he too was struggling with God and destiny, he was still a rich man's son and was fashionably dressed and riding a gaily caparisoned horse. Then suddenly his horse shied under him, and he looked up to see the sight that he most feared in all the world: a leper. Then happened for him, as for us also, a tremendous event, for Francis, fighting down his loathing and his fear, dismounted from his horse, and going to the leper, put money into his hand. Then impelled by some power that had overcome his fear, he took the hand and kissed it, putting his lips to the leper's flesh. And the leper, seeing that Francis was afire with love, took hold of him and gave him the kiss of peace and Francis kissed him also. Then Francis mounted his horse and rode back to Assisi with joy. From that day onward, he began to visit the lepers in the lazar house of Assisi, bringing them gifts and kissing their hands. He wrote in his will, "The Lord Himself led me amongst them, and I showed mercy to them, and when I left them, what had seemed bitter to me was changed into sweetness of body and soul."

*A Legend*: Francis remounted his horse and rode away. Then suddenly, he turned round, but there was no one to be seen on the road at all. Then he knew that he had kissed the Lord.

**Aldous Huxley**: Fear cannot be got rid of by personal effort, but only by the ego's absorption in a cause greater than its own interests. Absorption in any cause will rid the mind of some of its fears; but only absorption in the loving and knowing of the divine Ground can rid it of *all* fear. For when the cause is less than the highest, the sense of fear and anxiety is transferred from the self to the cause—as when heroic self-sacrifice for a loved individual or institution is accompanied by anxiety in regard to that for which the sacrifice is made. Whereas if the sacrifice is made for God, and for others for God's sake, there can be no fear or abiding anxiety, since nothing can be a menace to the divine Ground and even failure and disaster are to be accepted as being in accord with the divine will.[3]

## *PRAYER*

*O Lord, into Thy hands I commend my spirit, and the spirits of all those whom I love. Into Thy hands I commend the spirits of all those who are fearful, of death or life, of principalities or powers, of things present or of things that may never come. Into Thy hands I commend the spirits of all those who fear change, more than they fear Thee, who put the law above justice, and order above love.*

*And help me this coming day to do some work of peace for Thee.*

3. Aldous Huxley, *The Perennial Philosophy* (Cleveland, OH: The World Publishing Co., 1962), 163–164.

# 10

# PERFECT LOVE CASTS OUT FEAR

*There is no fear in love; but perfect love casts out fear.*
—1 John 4:18

The wisdom of the words of Aldous Huxley in the preceding meditation is profound. Only when our cause is the highest cause will all fear be conquered. For if our cause is not the highest cause, if it is a nation or a party or a movement or a church, and if it is this with which we identify ourselves, then the defeat of our cause is the defeat of ourselves. But if we believe that God is the ground of all being, we can accept defeat because in a sense, we cannot be defeated.

The conquest of fear is therefore a tremendous consequence of trying to find out what God's cause is—and making it our own. But there may be another tremendous consequence also. We may come into conflict with those institutions that view with suspicion—and sometimes with active hostility—any persons who have a supreme loyalty that is above their loyalty to party or movement or state or church, even though each of these bodies may call itself Christian. There is many a nation in the world—or, more accurately, there is many a national government in the world—that regards it as traitorous for a person to have a cause higher than that of the nation. If this nation calls itself Christian, it will argue that loyalty to God and loyalty to the nation are one and the same thing, and it will invent a Christian Nationalism in which one may have the best of both worlds. It will propound the proposition that only by being armed to the teeth can Christian civilization preserve itself. It may propound the even more extraordinary proposition that self-preservation must be the first law of a Christian, for if Christians do not preserve themselves, how can Christianity be preserved?

I live in a country where most of the white citizens would claim to be Christians, would feel it to be their supreme duty to preserve their Christian civilization, and sometimes, in moments of stress, would call it "white civilization." Many of them believe that God placed them in southern Africa to carry out a "civilizing mission." Most of them hold firmly the belief that this civilizing mission can only be carried out by the separation from one another of all racial groups—residentially, educationally, culturally, politically, even religiously.

I, for example, would have to receive a permit from the authorities if I wished to worship in a church that is situated in an African township or reserve, and this would only be granted for some special occasion. If I wished to worship there more often, it is almost certain that permission would be denied. Any Christian in South Africa who tried to break down the "middle wall of partition" between racial groups, or between persons of different racial groups, would find himself under suspicion, and this suspicion would vary, depending on his zeal. Any Christian or any other person who tried to break down the political wall of partition would not only find himself under suspicion but might find himself under house arrest, or banned from attending any meeting, or limited to some small area, or banished to some remote area, or detained without trial for a period that might be extended forever.

I write these words not with the trivial aim of bringing my government into disrepute, but with the aim of showing that if a Christian takes seriously the commandment to love his neighbor as himself, he may incur the active hostility of state and church. And we should remember that Jesus did exactly that, and He told His disciples that this might also happen to them. These sayings of Jesus should be taken seriously. Our Christian cause could well bring us into conflict with authority, and the only way we can overcome the fear of such a prospect is to believe that we are the instruments of God's peace—which means that we are the instruments of God's love, and because we are used by it, because it dwells in us, we have no cause for fear.

## *AN ADDENDUM*

The thoughts just concluded above are complete, and I did not wish to damage the unity of them by adding any observation that was not part of the main theme. Yet there is one observation that is important to me, and I make it now.

The observation is this: We may well be chary (or suspicious) of any person who makes the claim that his cause and God's cause are the same, who claims that he is in fact God's instrument. This claim may not be made explicitly, but may be implicit, as in the act of wearing a crucifix, or in the act of becoming a minister or priest, or in the act of accepting, say, an office in the parish or diocese. How is one to judge such claims, whether explicit or implicit?

How is one to judge such claimants? Is one able to do so? Yes, I believe one is, and the touchstone to use is the humility of the claimant. (But of the person or the church or the institution that makes such claims arrogantly, let us beware.)

At least one Christian showed this humility in an extraordinary way: After Francis had finally broken with his old life and had stripped himself of his gay[4] garments and handed them back to his father, declaring that he now had only one Father who was God, he was so filled with joy that he left Assisi and climbed up toward Gubbio, seeking the wildness and solitude and freedom of the mountains. When it was nearly evening, he happened by accident on a robbers' hideout, and they rushed out at him and demanded to know who he was and what was his business. Full of joy, he replied to them, "I am the herald of the Great King." So with loud laughter, they stripped off the cloak that Bishop Guido had given him and threw him into a snowdrift.

He crawled out of the snow, and dressed now only in his hairshirt, went singing on his way.

## *PRAYER*

*Give us courage, O Lord, to stand up and be counted, to stand up for those who cannot stand up for themselves, to stand up for ourselves when it is needful for us to do so. Let us fear nothing more than we fear Thee. Let us love nothing more than we love Thee, for thus we shall fear nothing also.*

*Let us have no other god before Thee, whether nation or party or state or church. Let us seek no other peace but the peace that is Thine and make us its instruments, opening our eyes and our ears and our hearts, so that we should know always what work of peace we may do for Thee.*

4. Meaning *fine* or *festive*.

# 11

# CARING FOR THE LEAST OF THESE

*Hear the word of the LORD, you rulers of Sodom; give ear to the law of our God, you people of Gomorrah. To what purpose is the multitude of your sacrifices to Me? says the LORD: I am full of the burned offerings of rams, and the fat of fed beasts; and I delight not in the blood of bullocks, or of lambs, or of he goats. When you come to appear before Me, who has required this at your hand, to tread My courts? Bring no more vain oblations; incense is an abomination to Me; the new moons and sabbaths, the calling of assemblies, I cannot away with; it is iniquity, even the solemn meeting. Your new moons and your appointed feasts My soul hates: they are a trouble to Me; I am weary to bear them. And when you spread forth your hands, I will hide My eyes from you: yea, when you make many prayers, I will not hear: your*

*hands are full of blood. Wash you, make you clean; put away the evil of your doings from before My eyes; cease to do evil; learn to do well; seek judgment, relieve the oppressed, judge the fatherless, plead for the widow. Come now, and let us reason together, says the* L*ORD*: *though your sins be as scarlet, they shall be as white as snow;*
*though they be red like crimson, they shall be as wool.*
—Isaiah 1:10–18

*Then shall the King say to them on His right hand, Come, you blessed of My Father, inherit the kingdom prepared for you from the foundation of the world: for I was hungry, and you gave Me meat* [food]: *I was thirsty, and you gave Me drink: I was a stranger, and you took Me in: naked, and you clothed Me: I was sick, and you visited Me: I was in prison, and you came to Me. Then shall the righteous answer Him, saying, Lord, when saw we You hungry, and fed You? or thirsty, and gave You drink? When saw we You a stranger, and took You in? or naked, and clothed You? Or when saw we You sick, or in prison, and came to You? And the King shall answer and say to them, Verily I say to you, Inasmuch as you have done it to one of the least of these My brethren, you have done it to Me.*
—Matthew 25:34–40

These two important passages make it clearer to us what God's cause is. It clearly has something to do with caring for others. If we do not care for or about others, then no amount of churchgoing, no number of observances, no amount of money given, *no amount of believing*, will give us any cause worth working for. In fact, one cannot believe in God in a religious sense unless one has this concern for others.

Now we may be shy or reserved and lacking in confidence, so that we cannot show love easily. We may feel indeed that we are being insincere if we try to do so. We may love Christ truly and deeply yet be austere by nature. Then let us accept ourselves as we are. It is not reserve but indifference, it is not shyness but coldness—these are the offenses against love. Let us heed the advice from "Desiderata" by Max Ehrmann: "Be yourself. Especially do not feign affection. Neither be cynical about love; for in the face of all aridity and disenchantment, it is as perennial as the grass."

It seems clear that the greatest offense is to be unloving. But love is not primarily giving expression to those tender feelings that are to be found in most human natures. It is primarily consenting to an orderliness of life and to a conscription of one's energy and talents. Love is not a sentimental thing, though I have known people calling themselves Christians to disparage it as such. To me, most of these people are afraid of love because they are afraid it might destroy their world.

To love means to bring one's whole life under discipline—extreme in the case of Francis, *wholesome* in the case of most others. This discipline, even if not extreme, means, negatively, refraining from any unloving or mean or cruel act, and positively, the offering of oneself to be made an instrument of God's peace.

## *CHRIST AND THE GRAND INQUISITOR*

In *The Brothers Karamazov*,[5] Fyodor Dostoevsky writes of the time of the Inquisition, when Christ is suddenly seen in the streets. He is recognized and brought to the Grand Inquisitor, who throws

5. Fyodor Dostoevsky, *The Brothers Karamazov* (New York: Random House, 1950).

Him into prison, intending to also kill Him. The Grand Inquisitor speaks to Him:

> I too prized the freedom with which Thou hast blessed men, and I too was striving to stand among Thy elect. … But I awakened and would not serve madness. I turned back and joined the ranks of those who have corrected Thy work. … I repeat, tomorrow Thou shalt see that obedient flock who at a sign from me will hasten to heap up the hot cinders about the pile on which I shall burn Thee for coming to hinder us. For if anyone ever deserved our fires, it is Thou. …
>
> When the Inquisitor ceased speaking he waited some time for his Prisoner to answer him. His silence weighed down upon him. He saw that the Prisoner had listened intently all the time, looking gently in his face and evidently not wishing to reply. The old man longed for Him to say something, however bitter and terrible. But He suddenly approached the old man in silence and softly kissed him on his bloodless, aged lips. That was all His answer. The old man shuddered. His lips moved. He went to the door, opened it, and said to Him, "Go, and come no more … come not at all, never, never." And he let Him out into the dark alleys of the town.

What does this story mean? It means for one thing that the church had become an end in itself, and in the name of Christ would break all the commandments of Christ, using the argument no doubt that if the church was not preserved, faith would die.

The story has a second meaning, not that Christ showed love to the Grand Inquisitor and so was released, but that Christ's manifestation of love was unendurable. In this story, love is not tenderness, it is judgment.

This is what others have told us about the nature of love:

**St. Teresa of Avila**: Let everyone understand that real love of God does not consist in tear-shedding, nor in that sweetness and tenderness for which usually we long, just because they console us, but in serving God in justice, fortitude of soul, and humility.

**William Law**: By love I do not mean any natural tenderness, which is more or less in people according to their constitution; but I mean a larger principle of the soul, founded in reason and piety, which makes us tender, kind, and gentle to all our fellow-creatures as creatures of God, and for His sake.

## *AN ANECDOTE*

Here is an anecdote that gives yet another manner of regarding love:

Dick Sheppard, the beloved, tempestuous, and eccentric vicar of St. Martin-in-the-Fields, was asked by a friend how he could possibly love a certain person, to which Sheppard replied, "I do more than love him; I positively like him!"

> O blessed Jesus, who knowest the impurity of our affection, the narrowness of our sympathy, and the coldness of our love, take possession of our souls and fill our minds with the image of Thyself. Break the stubbornness of our selfish wills and mold us in the likeness of Thine unchanging love, O Thou who only could, our Savior, our Lord, and our God.
>
> —**William Temple**

## *PRAYER*

*O Lord, help me to order my life better, help me to use my gifts more industriously, help me to turn from no one in need, help me to see You in the hungry, the sick, the prisoners, the lonely. Help me this coming day to do some work of peace for You.*

# 12

# THE LIGHT OF THE WORLD

*You are the light of the world.*
—Matthew 5:14

*I came not to judge the world, but to save the world.*
—John 12:47

*Because you are not of the world, but I have chosen you out of the world, therefore the world hates you.*
—John 15:19

*I pray not that You should take them out of the world, but that You should keep them from the evil.*
—John 17:15

*Love not the world, neither the things that are in the world.*
—1 John 2:15

*For God so loved the world...*
—John 3:16

These passages are confusing, especially to those who look to the Bible for guidance as to their conduct in every possible situation. In some passages, the world is the place to be lived in, to be redeemed, to be illuminated. In other passages, the world is irredeemable, the natural enemy of goodness and faith, a place not to be loved.

Some Christians, mostly members of sects, carry their shunning of the world to extreme lengths. In one of these sects, a man who is converted may no longer have any meaningful commerce with his wife if she is not converted. If a son or daughter is not converted by a certain age, he or she must be put out of the home. And what is more, a text can be found for it: "*I am come to set a man at variance against his father, and the daughter against her mother, and the daughter in law against her mother in law*" (Matthew 10:35).

What I hope to do here is to put down the thoughts of a Christian with no rigid belief, who nevertheless has all through his life pondered over these matters, who was brought up by parents who very much wanted their children to keep themselves unspoiled from the world. Alcohol was almost never seen in our home. My father smoked but not my mother ... but of course only a small percentage of the women of her generation smoked at all. We played card games, but never for money. We did not dance, go to the racetrack, or play games on Sunday. We went to the cinema but not to the theater! We were taught a rigid theology, and though it was important both to *believe* and to *do*, it was more important to *believe*. In later years, I caused my mother much anxiety by saying that if a person tried to lead a good and helpful life, I did not much care what he believed.

We were taught a strict obedience, both to God and to our parents. One of the things that irked us most was that in childhood, we were not allowed to go out of the house without supervision, unless to school or on some errand. Later this was relaxed, but our friends had to be approved and were in large part selected by my father.

Though we rebelled against many of those restrictions, we also learned to love the good, to be dutiful, to help those in need, to hate war and violence. When I went to college, I discovered that others had learned the same, with quite a different theology. From that time forward, I would have nothing more to do with any rigid system of belief. I married an Anglican girl and was attracted to Anglicanism because of its *wholesome discipline*. I became an Anglican, having shut my eyes and gritted my teeth and swallowed the Thirty-Nine Articles of Religion. Today going to the racetrack or drinking alcohol or going to the theater have no relevance to my idea of sin. One of my best friends is a race-going woman who has the same hopes for South Africa as I do and is not afraid to expose injustice when she finds it. Today the worst sins to me are cruelty and coldness. Cowardice is no doubt contemptible, but cruelty is horrible. And to me, the most horrible form of cruelty is that which men practice in order that some noble end may be achieved.

I have no higher vision of the church than as the servant of the world, not withdrawn but participating, not embattled but battling, not condemning but healing the wounds of the hurt and the lost and the lonely, not preoccupied with its survival or its observances or its articles, but with the needs of mankind.

Now this is often called the social gospel, the turning of the church into some kind of social welfare society, the exalting of the second commandment over what Jesus called *"the first and great commandment"* (Matthew 22:37–38). I think I can say something about this. During the Second World War, a wave of idealism surged through the South African armed forces in North Africa and Egypt, a determination to rid South Africa of those gross inequalities of status, wealth, and opportunity that so disfigure our society. This idealism had its counterpart at home, and one consequence of it was the appointment of a commission by Geoffrey Clayton, the great bishop of Johannesburg, to reexamine the state of our society and to make recommendations as to the kind of action the church and Christians should take. The report of the commission was presented to synod, and Clayton, who, as chairman, could never conceal his impatience, grew more and more restless as the discussion went on. At last, he could bear it no longer, and he jumped to his feet, obviously under the influence of great emotion, and emotion was something he was extremely suspicious of. His voice, always powerful, was now tremendous.

As I recall it, he said, "The church is not here primarily to serve society. Its prime duty is to worship God and obey Him. And if it is God's will that we should serve society in this or that way, then it is our duty to do it. Let us therefore be very careful that it is God's will we are trying to obey and that we are not merely trying to make the church do something that we want to be done. And let me make it quite clear that I appointed this commission because I believed it might be God's will that we should serve our society in this and that way." Then with a half-embarrassed, half-triumphant look, he ordered that discussion should proceed.

I have only one word to add to this, especially directed to those who do not have the sense of God's being and majesty that was so strong in Bishop Clayton, so strong that it was one of the few things that could evoke such emotion in him. If you do not have this sense, but wish to serve your society and your world, if you wish your life to be used for some purpose, then let your life be used and do not worry unduly about not having this sense. For some people, faith is preliminary to action; for others, action gives reality to faith; in most of us, sometimes one comes first, sometimes the other. I have no doubt that Francis kissed the leper because some tremendous faith was being born in him and that his faith was tremendously deepened by his act. In our own humble ways, may it be so with us.

> Here is thy footstool and there rest thy feet where live the poorest, and lowliest, and lost.
>
> When I try to bow to thee, my obeisance cannot reach down to the depth where thy feet rest among the poorest, and lowliest, and lost.
>
> Pride can never approach to where thou walkest in the clothes of the humble among the poorest, and lowliest, and lost.
>
> My heart can never find its way to where thou keepest company with the companionless among the poorest, the lowliest, and the lost.
>
> —Rabindranath Tagore (who was not a Christian)

**John Wesley**: Lord, let me not live to be useless.

13

# YOUR SINS ARE FORGIVEN

*And one of the Pharisees desired Him that He would eat with him. And He went into the Pharisee's house, and sat down to meat* [eat]. *And, behold, a woman in the city, which was a sinner, when she knew that Jesus sat at meat in the Pharisee's house, brought an alabaster box of ointment, and stood at His feet behind Him weeping, and began to wash His feet with tears, and did wipe them with the hairs of her head, and kissed His feet, and anointed them with the ointment. Now when the Pharisee which had bidden Him saw it, he spoke within himself, saying, This man, if He were a prophet, would have known who and what manner of woman this is that touches Him: for she is a sinner. And Jesus answering said to him, Simon, I have somewhat to say to you. And he says, Master, say on. There was a certain creditor which had two debtors: the one owed five hundred pence, and the other fifty. And when they had nothing to*

*pay, he frankly forgave them both. Tell me therefore, which of them will love him most? Simon answered and said, I suppose that he, to whom he forgave most. And He said to him, You have rightly judged. And He turned to the woman, and said to Simon, See you this woman? I entered into your house, you gave Me no water for My feet: but she has washed My feet with tears, and wiped them with the hairs of her head. You gave Me no kiss: but this woman since the time I came in has not ceased to kiss My feet. My head with oil you did not anoint: but this woman has anointed My feet with ointment. Wherefore I say to you, Her sins, which are many, are forgiven; for she loved much:*
*but to whom little is forgiven, the same loves little. And He said to her, Your sins are forgiven. And they that sat at meat with Him began to say within themselves, Who is this that forgives sins also? And He said to the woman, Your faith has saved you; go in peace.*

—Luke 7:36–50

There are several meanings to this story, but one is very clear—Simon judged, and Jesus forgave. Simon was no doubt an upright man, strict in observance, and very likely rich. We are not told what he thought of this woman coming uninvited into his house. But we are told that when the woman washed the feet of Jesus with her tears and kissed and anointed them, the first thought of Simon's was not of the ineffability of the scene that he was witnessing. His first thought was that Jesus, for all His reputations, did not know what kind of woman it was who was touching Him.

There is much of Simon in many of us who call ourselves Christians. When we are confronted by sinners—other than ourselves, I mean—we are often more inclined to judge than to forgive;

we are often more inclined to draw back than to go forward. Some kind of pride inhibits us, possibly some kind of fear. We do not wish to be seen associating with such persons.

When the sinner is repentant, such drawing back is unforgivable. The act of drawing back is then a far greater sin than the one that we are asked to forgive. The word *unforgiving* is one of the nastiest adjectives in the English language.

**"Love"**
**by George Herbert**
Love bade me welcome. Yet my soul drew back
Guilty of dust and sin.
But quick-eyed Love, observing me grow slack
From my first entrance in,
Drew nearer to me, sweetly questioning,
If I lacked any thing.

A guest, I answered, worthy to be here:
Love said, you shall be he.
I the unkind, ungrateful? Ah my dear,
I cannot look on thee.
Love took my hand, and smiling did reply,
Who made the eyes but I?

Truth Lord, but I have marred them: let my shame
Go where it doth deserve.
And know you not, says Love, who bore the blame?
My dear, then I will serve.
You must sit down, says Love, and taste my meat.
So I did sit and eat.

The pride, the strictness, and the lack of understanding of Simon the Pharisee, when they are found in us, not only create a vast gulf between ourselves and *sinners* but have in our time created a gulf between the old and the young. Older Christians are often repelled by the attitudes of the young toward sex, toward drugs, toward work. Alienation of another kind takes place when older Christians hold firm ideas about patriotism, loyalty, and fighting for one's country. Many young people reject war and violence, and they reject the world that cannot conduct its affairs without the use of war and violence. There is no doubt that many of them would refuse to take part if their country went to war. In my younger days, it required courage of a very high order to be a conscientious objector in times of war. Chairmen of tribunals could use almost any kind of insulting language to men asking to be exempted from war service. It was taken for granted that they were cowards. That is not the case today among the young.

It is often a matter of the utmost difficulty for older Christians to feel love for young people who appear to have rejected all the values of their elders, *and who are unrepentant about it.* Yet to some of these young people, Jesus is a hero. If only He were here now, many of them would flock to Him. In their disillusionment and lostness and anger at the world, have they not retained something of the gospel that we have lost, the knowledge that we must love one another? And when they came to Him, would they not see Him, not through a haze of marijuana darkly, but face to face, the brother whom they had lost and now had found again?

## *A HASIDIC STORY*

A father complained to the Baal Shem that his son had forgotten God. "What, rabbi, shall I do?" he asked. "Love him more than ever," was the Baal Shem's reply.

## *PRAYER*

*O Lord, teach us to humble ourselves before these children who live the gospel of love and drugs because we did not live the gospel of love. Teach us to humble ourselves before the problems that our children face in this generation. Especially we pray for all parents, that they may love their children steadfastly, even in the face of bewilderment and grief. Teach us to humble ourselves when we contemplate the world we have made, and the millions that we have killed and maimed in causes we believed to be just.*

*Above all, make us the instruments of Your love, so that even if we cannot help them, we shall still love them.*

*This we ask in the name of God who so loved the world, and of His Son Jesus, the lover of our souls.*

# 14

# BE NOT CONFORMED TO THIS WORLD

*Be not conformed to this world: but be you transformed by the renewing of your mind, that you may prove what is that good, and acceptable, and perfect, will of God.*
—Romans 12:2

It is one of the good signs of our times that there is such self-criticism within the church. This self-criticism is practiced by both clergy and laity. It is very different from the criticism of those who are outside the church and would not particularly want the church to succeed in practicing what it preaches. Nor is it the same as the criticism of those who are members of the church, who perpetually criticize the church and especially the clergy because it is their scapegoat for their own failures.

By this I mean the criticism of those who are fully in the church, who are distressed by the way it often adapts itself to the *pattern of this present world,* who want to see it a witness for Christ in the world. The trouble with witnessing for Christ in the world is that it is at times almost impossible not to antagonize the rich, the well-established, the ruling classes, and important people within the church itself. If a priest or minister does so, he is stigmatized as a *political parson.* Instead of sticking to his work of saving souls, he is *dragging politics into religion.* By challenging the pattern of this present world, he is undermining law and order and is ignoring Paul's advice to the Romans:

> *Let every soul be subject to the higher powers. For there is no power but of God: the powers that be are ordained of God. Whosoever therefore resists the power, resists the ordinance of God: and they that resist shall receive to themselves damnation. For rulers are not a terror to good works, but to the evil. Will you then not be afraid of the power? do that which is good, and you shall have praise of the same: for he is the minister of God to you for good. But if you do that which is evil, be afraid; for he bears not the sword in vain: for he is the minister of God, a revenger to execute wrath upon him that does evil. Wherefore you must needs be subject, not only for wrath, but also for conscience sake. For this cause pay you tribute also: for they are God's ministers, attending continually upon this very thing.* (Romans 13:1–6)

I am one of those Christians who find it impossible to reconcile Romans 12:2 and Romans 13:1–6. In this second passage, St. Paul seems to suggest that the existing authorities are the guardians of morality, and that if we do right, we need not fear the authorities. St. Paul's life and death were irrefutable proofs that this is not true. Jesus was crucified by the existing authorities, who were

God's agents. Nothing in the teachings of Jesus suggests that to follow Him will ensure a quiet life, acceptable to the powers that be. I myself have friends of what is called *unimpeachable character* who are restricted in movement and are not allowed to attend any social gathering because they did not adapt themselves to the pattern of their present world.

When Peter and others had angered the high priest by their teaching, they were brought before the Sanhedrin:

> *The high priest asked them, saying, Did not we strictly command you that you should not teach in this name? and, behold, you have filled Jerusalem with your doctrine, and intend to bring this man's blood upon us. Then Peter and the other apostles answered and said, We ought to obey God rather than men.* (Acts 5:27–29)

The belief that the church must never challenge the state, except in extreme cases that seldom arise, is deeply rooted in many parts of the church. The belief that the church must challenge the state if the state embarks on any action that runs counter to Christ's teaching is also deeply rooted. This leads to compromises, not only within the church but between church and state.

**William Temple:** One of the commonest of the compromises that have been made is for the world to allow the church to be at peace in proclaiming what may be called its philosophical paradoxes provided that it keeps quiet about its moral ones.

Not for one moment must we underestimate the immense problem of the coexistence of church and state, nor the problem of how to follow the teachings of Jesus in a secular society. It is no answer to say we must be more loving.

Francis faced the same problem. While on a preaching mission in the foothills of the Apennines, he heard that there was to be a tournament at Montefeltro Castle. Although he had left the pleasures of the world, he decided to go to the tournament and mingled happily with the gay, cheerful crowd. At some point, he climbed on to some seat or pillar and asked for silence so that he might speak. Then he preached to them of the heavenly country, touching their hearts. When he had finished, one of the great nobles, Lord Orlando dei Cattani, asked if they could speak together, and Francis agreed willingly to do so when the noble lord had done his social duties. And what did Lord Orlando ask him? Something that we might have asked him too, for he wanted to know not how to join the order, but how to live the Christian life in the world. And when Francis said he would help him, Orlando asked him to accept a gift for his order, which was nothing less than the mountain of Alvernia in the Apennines, where Francis later received the five wounds.

Thus was born at Montefeltro the Third Order, for those who had lives to live and duties to do in the world. Christians in the world had first to love God, to praise Him, to practice prayer, and be obedient to God's commandments. They were to love their neighbors as themselves and to be the servants of all, remembering especially the poor. They were to accord justice to all and to practice mercy. They were to be charitable to their enemies, honest in business, moderate in the use of food and drink and clothes, disciplined in life, and self-denying. They were to be loyal to the church, observing its rites, taking part in its fasts and its feasts, especially the blessed sacrament, repenting them of their sins, and receiving God with a pure heart and chaste body.

Francis wrote all these things down in his "Letter to All Christians," and this letter formed the basis of the Rule of the Third Order. Such a man as Lord Orlando, who was one of the first to be admitted, continued to administer his estates as before, but with a new hope and aim. Rich merchants eschewed luxury.

The Third Order was the answer to many who needed guidance as to how to live in the world without conforming to the accepted pattern of things.

## *AN ADDENDUM (THE AUTHOR GREATLY DARING)*

There is no such thing as *saving souls* unless we save them for something. We cannot save them for God, because they are His already. But we may save them for some purpose of God. We may save them by inspiring them—not to belong to God, which they already do, but to become His instruments, thus making themselves part of the divine creativity that rules the world. If a soul makes itself part of that, then it is saved. A Christian may believe, as we have seen earlier, that certain of our social arrangements are such as to make it almost impossible for a man to conceive himself as part of the divine creativity, or to take part in his work, which means, of course, that he cannot realize himself as a man. If a Christian wishes to work for the removal of such impediments, then he is not bringing politics into religion, he is trying to save souls for the purpose for which they were created.

**Russian philosopher Nikolai Berdyaev:** The present state of the world calls for a moral and spiritual revolution, revolution in the name of personality, of men, of every single person. This revolution should restore the hierarchy of values, now quite shattered, and place the value of human personality above the idols of production, technics, the state, race, nationality, the collective.

**The Prayer of Toc H:** O God, ... teach us to live together in love and joy and peace; to check all bitterness; to disown discouragement; to practice thanksgiving: and to leap with joy to any task for others. Strengthen the good thing thus begun; that with gallant and high-hearted happiness we may work for Thy kingdom in the wills of men. Through Jesus Christ our Lord.

**Reinhold Niebuhr**: God, grant me the serenity to accept the things I cannot change, courage to change the things I can, and the wisdom to know the difference.

## *PRAYER*

*O Lord, grant that we may not be conformed to the world, but may love it and serve it. Grant we may never shrink from being the instruments of Thy peace because of the judgment of the world. Grant that we may love Thee without fear of the world; grant that we may never believe that the inexpressible majesty of Thyself may be found in any power of this earth. May we firstly love Thee and our neighbors as ourselves. May we remember the poor and the prisoner and the sick and the lonely, and the young searchers, and the tramps and vagabonds, and the lost and the lonely, as we remember Christ, who is in them all. And may we this coming day be able to do some work of peace for Thee.*

15

# LET ME BRING JOY

*Where there is sorrow, let me bring joy;*
*where there is darkness, light.*
—Prayer of St. Francis

A university president from the United States was on a visit to South Africa, and he made a special point of visiting with me. When he returned to America, he wrote to me, telling me that I was not the kind of person he had expected to see. I replied and asked him what he meant, and he wrote back that he had expected to see me more a man of joy, and what he meant was, a man of Christian joy.

This observation, which was as sharp and clean as a knife, led me to do some thinking, and although I do not wish to obtrude myself unduly in this book, I cannot escape it now.

Why can I not be described as joyful? Why on the whole can my friends not be described as joyful? Most of them have a decided sense of humor, and all of them have experienced joyful occasions, reunions, blessings, and achievements, and expect to experience many more. People have been known to shout for joy, leap for joy, dance for joy, weep for joy. All these things they do on *joyous occasions*. Some of the most spectacular joyous occasions are those in which our cause has triumphed, and someone else's cause has been defeated!

These joyous occasions I understand well. I have often experienced them. I have often been able to be the bringer of joy to others; this is a country in which small things, small gifts, small recognitions, small identifications, can bring disproportionate joy. Not only does one bring joy, one experiences joy in bringing it. And the reason is that when one brings joy, and when one experiences joy in bringing it, one has what I can only describe as an experience of God. I am not speaking of mystical experience, because I do not have much mystical experience. What I am speaking of, to coin a pretty terrible phrase, is the joy of instrumentality. The more I am used as an instrument, the closer do I approach a state of abiding joy.

The world, however, is a tough place. It brings frustrations, and frustrations in this context mean that one's instrumentality is restricted in its scope by forces that one does not control. This calls for fortitude, patience, and constancy. These are the qualities of the friends with whom I have worked. Not for a moment do I suppose that they are the only ones who have them, nor do I suppose that those who are opposed to me do not have them.

Now I think it is quite possible that the espousal of a cause that one believes to be worthy of one's devotion—the facing of difficulties with fortitude, patience, and constancy, the willingness to endure suffering for the sake of this cause—can bring joy. Instantly there comes to my mind the famous photograph of Mahatma Gandhi and Jawaharlal Nehru sitting together on a mat, with Gandhi the picture of childlike gaiety, which is a manifestation of joy. That Jesus could be cheerful, I could not for a moment question, though the Gospels do not tell us about it; they tell us much more about the graver joy of a hard course chosen and pursued to the end.

Therefore, while I wish I could be more joyous and do more of this shouting, leaping, dancing, and weeping, I shall tell myself to accept myself, which as everyone knows, is dangerous advice. I shall not take too desperate a view of my own situation. I remember, though not well, one of the well-known stories of World War II, told of the man who was responsible for the safety of British merchant shipping. This man I shall call Sir John, but that was probably not his name. Things were going pretty badly for British shipping, and one of Sir John's colleagues was in his office, filling the air with gloom.

Sir John said to him sharply, "You've forgotten Rule No. 4?"

His colleague asked with surprise, "What's Rule No. 4?"

"Rule No. 4," said Sir John, "is 'Don't take yourself too seriously.'"

His colleague asked, "What are the other rules?"

Sir John replied, "There aren't any others."

So I shall try—and those like me should try too—not to take too serious a view of our failure to attain this state of permanent joy. St. Francis did it, but as someone said to me reproachfully, "St. Francis was a saint!" Yet he too passed through a long period of what could only be called an absence of joy.

This year, a friend of mine wished me a happy Easter, and I, because my wife was gravely ill, replied that I did not think it would be happy. When he reached home, he sat down and wrote to me that no Christian should be unhappy at Easter because what had happened at Easter was of an eternal order, whereas our griefs were temporal.

I replied to him that I did not expect to be unhappy at Easter. I was prepared to face the future and whatever it might bring. I wrote, "I like to see happiness and to see happy people, especially happy children. I hope they may grow up happy also, but if I had to choose, I would rather see them brave."

And many of those I know have had to choose. They do not show the outward signs of joy, but they have an inner fortitude, a kind of inner equilibrium that has cost too much to be tranquility and is still too much on guard to be serenity. I think that such an inner equilibrium might possibly be called joy.

Suppose that one experienced a deep personal grief, just at Eastertime. Could one be happy as well? I try not to think in these categories at all. The grief will go, the deeper fortitude will stay. And this fortitude comes from the faith that the things we believe in and the things we try to do are right.

## *PRAYER*

*Make me, O Lord, the instrument of Thy love, that I may bring comfort to those who sorrow and joy to those who are regarded as persons of little account. In this country of many races, make me courteous to those who are humble and understanding to those who are resentful. Teach me what I should be to the arrogant and cruel, for I do not know.*

*And as for me myself, make me more joyful than I am, especially if this is needed for the sake of others. Let me remember my many experiences of joy and thankfulness, especially those that endure. And may I this coming day do some work of peace for Thee.*

16

# LET ME CONSOLE, UNDERSTAND, AND LOVE

*O Divine Master, grant that I may not so much seek to be consoled, as to console; not so much to be understood, as to understand; not so much to be loved, as to love.*
—Prayer of St. Francis

It is about seventeen years since I first read the prayer that is the subject of these meditations. Why I had never seen it before, I do not know. Since that time, I have met more and more people who know it and who find that it speaks to them firmly and clearly in these shifting times. I suppose it would be true to say that no religion in the world has become so entangled with dogma and doctrine and creed as has our own. The great commandments are two. The first is to love God with heart and soul and mind; the second is to love our neighbors as ourselves. "*On these two commandments hang all the law and the prophets*" (Matthew 22:40). And let us remember, there are many people who have been led to understand and obey the first commandment because they tried to be obedient to the second.

**St. Teresa of Avila:** We cannot know whether we love God, although there may be strong reasons for thinking so, but there can be no doubt about whether we love our neighbors or no. Be sure that in proportion as you advance in fraternal charity, you are increasing in your love of God, for His Majesty bears so tender an affection for us, that I cannot doubt He will repay our love for others by augmenting, in a thousand different ways, that which we bear for Him.

What more encouraging words could there be than these, especially for those who love the good and are searching for the God from whom all good comes? What encouragement to be told by a saint that "we cannot know whether we love God, although there may be strong reasons for thinking so"! I am attracted to many people who love the good and live their lives as though under some obedience; and I find that they in their turn are attracted to those Christians who try to obey the two great commandments. Whatever else shifts, these two do not shift. On them all else is built—morality, theology, ideals, principles. Yet nothing that is built on them must ever supersede them. If they are ever superseded, then we get that loveless Christianity that is more concerned with law, authority, abstentions, and observances than with the prisoner in the prison house. I know this Christianity, I have sat in councils with it. Its face is too terrible to look upon. No wonder Jesus had such a love for sinners.

The first petition of St. Francis—that he should be the instrument of God's peace—is the greatest that any Christian can offer, and it is followed by six sub-petitions, each of them elements of the first, each sublime in its intention. And no sooner have we been overwhelmed by it than it is followed by a second petition of equal power, that one should seek not so much to be consoled as to console, a petition offered with a purity and a humility that move me as deeply as I write now as ever they did before. Yet Francis does not say that he does not wish to be consoled, understood, and loved. He is willing to receive, for if he is not willing to receive, then he is preventing someone from giving.

That is what Peter once tried to do; he tried to prevent someone from giving.

> *Jesus knowing that the Father had given all things into His hands, and that He was come from God, and went to God; He rose from supper, and laid aside His garments; and took a towel, and girded Himself. After that He poured water into a basin, and began to wash the disciples' feet, and to wipe them with the towel wherewith He was girded. Then came He to Simon Peter: and Peter said to Him, Lord, do You wash my feet? Jesus answered and said to him, What I do you know not now; but you shall know hereafter. Peter said to Him, You shall never wash my feet. Jesus answered him, If I wash you not, you have no part with Me. Simon Peter said to Him, Lord, not my feet only, but also my hands and my head. ... So after He had washed their feet, and had taken His garments, and was set down again, He said to them, Know you what I have done to you? You call Me Master and Lord: and you say well; for so I am. If I then, your Lord and Master, have washed your feet; you also ought to wash one another's feet. For I have given you an example, that you should do as I have done to you. Verily, verily, I say to you, The servant is not greater than his lord; neither he that is sent greater than he that sent him. If you know these things, happy are you if you do them.* (John 13:3–9, 12–17)

In my own country, where there are many races, and where race difference is established and maintained by law, it is difficult for many members of the so-called superior groups to serve those of the so-called inferior groups. For every white man who would help an old black woman to cross a busy street, there would be some who would not, though perhaps some of those would wish that they *could* do so. But once the barrier is crossed, the whole personality becomes richer and gentler. There is only one way in which man's inhumanity to man can be made endurable to us, and that is when we in our own lives try to exemplify man's humanity to man.

It sometimes happens in this country that a poor person brings a gift to one who is not poor. If it is done in love and kindness or gratitude, then it should be received. Let us seek not so much to be consoled as to console, but when it is our turn to be consoled, then let us receive such consolation with humility and thanks.

**St. Ignatius of Loyola**: Teach us, good Lord, to serve Thee as Thou deservest; to give and not to count the cost; to fight and not to heed the wounds; to toil and not to ask for rest; to labor and not to ask for any reward, save that of knowing that we do Thy will. Through Jesus Christ our Lord.

# 17

# REAPING WHAT WE HAVE SOWN

Racial warfare flared in Detroit again yesterday, and the death toll rose to 35. There had been a few hours of calm—during which Black leaders threatened guerilla warfare and said: "We stand on the eve of a Black revolution." Violence also flared in another seven Michigan cities yesterday—Saginaw, Grand Rapids, Pontiac, Flint, Muskegon, Benton Harbor and Mount Clemens.

*The Natal Mercury*, Durban, South Africa
Morning edition, July 27, 1967

2000 crack American paratroopers, some just back from Vietnam, are still guarding East Detroit. Rioting continued last night in Toledo, Cincinnati, Chicago, Cambridge (Maryland), San Francisco and Phoenix. At least 20

> people were arrested in Toledo after Negroes had thrown fire bombs and looted shops.
>
> *The Daily News*, Durban, South Africa
> Evening edition, July 27, 1967

> Tired Federal troops finally curbed America's costliest-ever riots in Detroit yesterday, but more Negro violence exploded in other cities across the country. In Los Angeles, fire-bombs were thrown in the streets of the Watts section—a grim reminder of the six-day 1965 riots there in which 35 people died. Guardsmen used riot gas in Cambridge, Maryland, to disperse 400 Negroes who had gathered for a street rally. The town was the scene of a violent riot two days ago.
>
> *The Natal Mercury*, July 28, 1967

> Stokely Carmichael has issued from Havana a threat of Black vengeance. … "We are not waiting for them to kill us. We will move to kill them first, or rather, we are working towards that goal. … One good thing about the Vietnam war is that the United States has taught us how to kill. Our brothers returning from Vietnam are going to use that training well in the cities of the United States."
>
> *The Natal Mercury*, August 3, 1967

When I read this news, my heart aches, not only for America but for myself too. Why is there all this depth of hatred, and when did it begin? It had several sources, and slavery is certainly one of them. In the fifteenth, sixteenth, seventeenth, eighteenth, and even nineteenth century after Christ, the ships of Europe carried slaves from Africa to the New World. In 1790, according to the *Encyclopaedia Britannica*, 74,000 Africans were forcibly removed from the west coast of Africa. Of these, one-eighth would die on the journey, one twentieth die in the harbor, and one-third die in the "seasoning." It is estimated by some that twenty million Africans were abducted from Africa during the life of the trade. Some fell into the hands of humane masters; some lived lives of unspeakable misery, suffering the extremes of cruelty and degradation. All lived the lives of slaves.

**Abraham Lincoln**, in his second inaugural address: Fondly do we hope—fervently do we pray—that this mighty scourge of war may speedily pass away. Yet, if God wills that it continue until all the wealth piled by the bondsman's two hundred and fifty years of unrequited toil shall be sunk and until every drop of blood drawn with the lash shall be paid by another drawn with the sword, as it was said three thousand years ago, so still it must be said "the judgments of the Lord are true and righteous altogether."

Lincoln certainly would have called these riots judgments of the Lord. The harvest we are reaping comes from the seed that we have sowed. What must be done now? Clearly the main task falls to the authorities to create that kind of society in which hatred will die away—because when there is hope, purpose, and recognition, then hatred does die away. This society has been called the Great Society, but no great society will ever be built as long as there exist gross inequalities of income, opportunity, and status. To remove these is going to cost a lot of money, a lot of thought, a lot of work. We shall never build the Great Society so long as we pour our money into armaments. And what is hardest of all, we shall have to endure hatred while we are building it. While we are building it, we are going to be hated, cursed, stoned, shot at, perhaps even killed, by some of the very people for whom we are building it. We are going to have to go on building while we are being hated.

I doubt whether any nation has ever before been faced with such a task.

*But it has to be undertaken.* The alternatives are unthinkable. One alternative would be to partition the United States of America. The other would be to go back to segregation, to the shooting, lynching, hanging—back to real segregation, with stockades, gates, barbed wire, floodlights, armed guards, machine guns, death rays, and if that doesn't solve the problem, back to the gas chambers. America cannot go back one inch on that road. So great is the crisis confronting her that she would be justified in organizing a great army, not to fight the enemies abroad but those at home, using all the energy and idealism of her young people, many of whom would willingly devote their lives to such a cause, many of whom are now rebels without any cause at all.

When I face some problem whose solution seems impossible, I always think of London on October 15, 1940, when 480 German aircraft dropped an estimated 386 tons of high explosive and 70,000 incendiary bombs. The incendiary bombs were something new, and while Londoners sheltered in the basements, strategic and historic buildings burned out above their heads. If this were to go on night after night, nothing of London would be left. And what could Londoners possibly do? "'To the basements,'" wrote Churchill, "must be replaced by 'To the roofs.'" What had seemed a hopeless future became an inspiring present. Everyone pressed forward to do his or her share. "Many became adept," wrote Churchill, "and thousands of fires were extinguished before they took hold. The experience of remaining on the roof night after night under fire, with no protection but a tin hat, soon became habitual."

What Londoners did then, we must do now, because people are threatening to "burn America down."

And what must *I* do, apart from what I do as a citizen enrolled by my government at a time of national crisis, or as a member of some civic group or church or another group? I must try to understand what makes people hate, loot, and kill. If I am white, then I must try to understand the consequences of that amazing intellectual flowering of the West, accompanied by technological advances that enabled the people and nations of Europe to go into every country of the world and virtually to do what they liked, even to the extent of annexing whole countries that belonged to other people, that tremendous historical process known as colonization, which was as catastrophic in its undoing as it was in its doing, so catastrophic that it will take the world generations to recover from it all. If I am tempted to point to African wars, I must remember World War I and World War II, and the massacre of the Jews by Adolf Hitler. If I am tempted to sneer at Congo chaos, then I must remember who prepared the way for it. If I am angered by Congo brutality, then let me also remember King Leopold II of Belgium. If I am tempted to hate and if I fall to the temptation, then I repent, or I cease to be a Christian.

There is only one thing I can do in times like these, when some people—and some of them very intelligent people—fear a total estrangement between black and white. Then I, whether I am black or white, must ask to be made an instrument of God's peace, so that one more healing stream may flow into the river of hate. It is hard for me to see God's power working in these dangerous times, unless it works through us.

In April 1958, when Dag Hammarskjöld was beginning his second term as secretary-general of the United Nations, the staff gave him a surprise party, and he made a speech of thanks. He concluded, author Henry P. Van Dusen tells us, with a favorite verse from the Swedish poet Gunnar Ekelöf: "Will the day ever come when joy is great and sorrow small?" Hammarskjöld added his own answer: "On the day we feel we are living with a duty, well fulfilled and worth our while, on that day, joy is great, and we can look on sorrow as being small."

## *PRAYER*

> *Lord, strengthen us in these troublous times. Save us from a retreat into hatred or despair. Call us out of the shelters and send us up to the roofs, even if day and night we are under fire. Help us to rebuild the house that is broken down and to put out the flames before they destroy us all. Rebuke us for any self-pity and teach us rather to keep our pity for others who need it. May we remain calm in the midst of violence and panic. May reason, love, mercy, and understanding rule our lives. And may we this coming day be able to do some work of peace for Thee.*

18

# IT IS IN GIVING THAT WE RECEIVE

*For it is in giving that we receive.*
—Prayer of St. Francis

If you love, you will be loved;

If you respect people, you will be respected;

If you serve them, you will be served;

If you give a good account of yourself toward others, others will act likewise toward you.

Blessed is the man who loves and does not desire to be loved for it;

> Blessed is he who respects others and does not look for respect in return;
>
> Who serves and does not expect service for it; who acquits himself well of others and does not desire that they return the grace.
>
> Because such things are big, foolish people do not rise to them.
>
> —**Brother Giles of Assisi**

No one has ever found a satisfactory explanation of the source of the prayer of St. Francis. The saying of Brother Giles given above is obviously akin to the prayer and may well have been inspired by it, for Brother Giles joined the Franciscan order in 1209 and was a member of it for over fifty years until his death in 1262. This has led some to think that he knew the prayer, and that he knew it because it was composed by St. Francis.

The meaning of the saying is clearly, "It is in giving that we receive, and blessed is he who gives without thought of receiving." I venture to think that St. Francis meant that quite apart from any expectation or lack of it, in giving we *do* receive. We cannot do anything but receive because that is a law of our being. There is only one condition attached to it, and that is that when we give, it must be ourselves that we are giving. The gift, the money, the book, the flowers, are only symbols in this kind of giving; they are signs that it is ourselves that we are giving.

It is not uncommon in a society where there is great disparity of wealth for the *haves* to argue among themselves as to whether the *have-nots* are grateful or ungrateful. Some *haves* are obsessed with a belief in the ingratitude of the *have-nots,* to the extent that they are embittered by it. "I gave him this and I gave him that and look what he did to me!" That there are cases of ingratitude one cannot doubt, but apart from those, it is my experience that those who complain of ingratitude never give *themselves* with their gifts. It is the gift, the thing, the money, that they expect to evoke the response, and very often, it does not. But when we give ourselves, not seeking gratitude, we are often overwhelmed by the response in some other person who at that moment gives himself to us. It is in that moment that we receive; it is in that moment that God *is*; it is in that place that God is. That, above all, is what we receive, and it is an experience of joy. And that, for me, is one of the meanings of God, that He is in that time and place where you and I give ourselves to each other.

Sometimes it happens that I give myself and you take, but you do not give yourself. This often happens in love between man and woman. Far from bringing joy, it brings pain. Sometimes it happens that I give myself, and you will not even take. This happened to Jesus and drew from Him the cry, "*O Jerusalem, Jerusalem, you that kill the prophets, and stone them which are sent to you, how often would I have gathered your children together, even as a hen gathers her chickens under her wings, and you would not!*" (Matthew 23:37). Yet one cannot read the fourteenth, fifteenth, sixteenth, and seventeenth chapters of St. John's Gospel without realizing that in giving greatly, so did Jesus receive. Did He not say:

> *Give, and it shall be given to you; good measure, pressed down, and shaken together, and running over, shall men give into your bosom. For with the same measure that you mete withal [measure anything] it shall be measured to you again.*
>
> (Luke 6:38)

One of the most tragic characters I have ever met was a priest who had spent the greater part of his life as a missionary in

Swaziland[6] and came to Johannesburg to retire. When I asked him about his life among the Swazis, to my astonishment, his mouth began to quiver with pain and his eyes to fill with tears. He said to me with a mixture of anger and hurt, "I do not like to speak about it; they are the most ungrateful people in the world." Something had gone wrong with the manner of giving.

Compare this with the story of the Curé d'Ars, St. John Vianney. He was a dunce at school and distressed his parents by deciding to become a priest. So deep was his devotion that the authorities virtually pushed him through the seminary, and in his first parish, the vicar thought him too stupid to let him preach. But the bishop had more insight and appointed him curé or parish pastor of Ars, France. From this small parish, his fame slowly spread throughout all France. Hundreds of thousands of people, great and small, made their pilgrimage to Ars to hear him preach, to touch him, to confess to him, to be absolved, to be blessed. When he left his church to go to his room, so great was the crowd, so urgent their demands, that it took him thirty minutes to cross the square. He was canonized in 1925, some sixty-six years after his death, and in 1929, he was made the patron saint of parish priests. He gave abundantly of what appeared to be the most humble gifts and also received in abundance. Even the unbelieving world recognized in him the instrument of some supreme Power.

What does giving oneself to God mean? Whatever else it means, it certainly means giving oneself to others.

## *PRAYER*

*Lord, help me to give myself when I am giving. Teach me to give without thought of receiving and to receive without thought of giving. Teach me not to withhold or to withdraw*

6. Now the Kingdom of Eswatini.

*myself. Teach me to hoard nothing—not love, money, time, or possessions. Make me ready to give even my life if it is required of me. And while I have it, use it as an instrument of Your peace.*

# 19

# AS WE FORGIVE

*It is in pardoning that we are pardoned.*
—Prayer of St. Francis

We have discussed the subject of forgiveness, but not the implication of the petition in the Lord's Prayer, "*Forgive us the wrong we have done, as we have forgiven those who have wronged us*" (Matthew 6:12 NEB). Jesus goes on, after the prayer is ended, to say, "*For if you forgive others the wrongs they have done, your heavenly Father will also forgive you; but if you do not forgive others, then the wrongs you have done will not be forgiven by your Father*" (Matthew 6:14–15 NEB).

How is this to be interpreted? I know that in trying to interpret, I lay myself open to the charge that I interpret things the way I like them to be.

These are my difficulties:

1. It sounds as if Jesus is saying, "If you do this, then God will do that; but if you don't, He won't either." I find this hard to believe of God, who causes His rain to fall on both the just and the unjust.
2. When Jesus said, *"Father, forgive them; for they know not what they do"* (Luke 23:34), He seems to imply a forgiveness that is freely given, even to those who have not repented.
3. It is my reading of "love your enemies and pray for your persecutors" (see Matthew 5:44) that we are being enjoined to love them and pray for them, even when they have not repented or do not have any intention of repenting. And surely we cannot love them if we have not forgiven them. If this can be expected of us, how may we expect less of God?

Greatly daring, I would venture this interpretation: If you do not forgive those who have wronged you, then your heavenly Father will not be able to forgive you, for you will never be able to recognize forgiveness so long as you have not forgiven these others.

It seems to me that there are at least two kinds of forgiveness. There is one kind in which one person forgives another, but the forgiven person does not know and may not care that he has been forgiven. A son who has caused his mother much grief may at last repent and ask for forgiveness, and the mother may well reply, "Son, I forgave you long ago." This kind of forgiveness was shown by the father of the prodigal son, who saw his son when he was still a great way off and ran and fell on his neck and kissed him. (See Luke 15:20.) Yet even in this first kind of forgiveness, which is very wonderful, the relationship is only restored when, and does not exist until, the second person has repented.

The other kind of forgiveness is that in which the second person first repents and is then forgiven. This frequently happens between husband and wife; the one hurts the other and after a time, when pride has come to its senses, says, "I am sorry," and the relationship is immediately restored.

Now it seems to me that God may well forgive us while we are still a great way off, and perhaps not even on the way home at all. *But for us ourselves, it is essential that we ask for forgiveness; otherwise we shall not recognize or experience it.* It is essential that we should have forgiven others, for our relationship with others is one way of knowing God. We cannot hope to be instruments of God's peace when we ourselves are not at peace with others, and certainly not when we hate them.

> *If you bring your gift to the altar, and there remember that your brother has anything against you; leave there your gift before the altar, and go your way; first be reconciled to your brother, and then come and offer your gift.*
>
> (Matthew 5:23–24)

In a small town near the place where I live, a young married man killed and mutilated a young girl with whom he had been having a love affair. For this, he was sentenced to death; and while he was awaiting execution, the parents of the dead girl let it be known through the medium of the newspapers that they had forgiven him. This action was generally considered a noble one, even by those who said that they themselves could never have taken it.

Furthermore it is generally considered churlish in a person if he refuses forgiveness to one who asks for it. I have had this experience. When I was a young schoolmaster, I looked after some seventy boys in one wing of the school hostel, and the senior matron was responsible for about the same number of girls in the other wing. One afternoon when I returned from school, I found that the matron had shut two small girls in a cupboard for some offense or other. In my anger, I told her that her action was disgraceful, after which she would not speak to me. The atmosphere in our common dining room was decidedly unpleasant, and when the second matron advised me to apologize, I did so. However, the senior matron refused to accept my apology, and for two long years, we ate our meals at the same table and never exchanged a word with each other. In fact, she became my enemy. She became actively hostile to anything I did or said. Did I love her? I certainly did not. For me, she was the apotheosis of astringent spinsterhood.

I think it is true to say that in South Africa, the gulf between white apartheiders and their opponents is wide and deep, as wide and deep a gulf as exists in any country. The differences are political but moral too. The apartheiders think that their opponents, especially their white ones, are traitors to the country, agitators, communists, or liberals, which is just as bad because liberals in their fatuous sentimentality open the gates for the communists to enter the holy city. The opponents think that many of the policies of apartheid are cruel and indifferent to human suffering, and that many apartheiders know this, but think the ideal of racial separation so noble as to justify such means. What is more, the apartheiders wield tremendous temporal power and their opponents none, and this power is used to ban, banish, silence, and forbid social intercourse to those who are most active in opposition.

Thus the relationship that exists is virtually one of enmity. I just do not know how else to describe it. *I should like to place on record that I do not hate my opponents.* I also must place on record that I do not love them, not in any sense of the word *love* as I know it.

If "*love your enemies*" means "regard your enemies as children of God and treat them with humanity," then I would understand it, but it would still be an evasion to me.

I do not quite know why I do not hate my enemies. I know from experience that hate is corrosive, and that one who hates does terrible damage to his own character and personality. But I doubt whether one can refrain from feeling so powerful an emotion just because one has such experiential knowledge. I can only thank God that I am not given to hating. What is more, I thank God for the knowledge that one becomes less and less given to hating as one becomes more and more given to loving.

I close with a last observation. When I read Matthew, chapter 23, I find it hard to believe that Jesus loved the legalists and the Pharisees and the hypocrites. Had one of them come to Him seeking, as Nicodemus did, I do not doubt that He would have loved him. If Jesus *did* love the legalists and the Pharisees and the hypocrites, then He loved them in some sense of the word *love* that I do not understand.

James B. Pratt, in *India and Its Faiths*, tells the story of the Indian who, at the time of the Indian Mutiny, greeted the soldier about to bayonet him with the extraordinary words, "And thou too art divine." That this is sublime, who would question? And I read into it the meaning that the man about to die is in that moment at one with the Divine, so that his love reaches out even to the man who is about to kill him. I conclude that the nearer one is to the Divine, the more one is able to love one's enemies, and that I myself am far from it, though I wish to be nearer.

## *PRAYER*

> *Lord, teach me the meaning of Your commandment to love our enemies and help me to obey it. Make me the instrument of Your love, which is not denied to the hungry, the sick, the prisoner, the enemy.*

*Teach me to hate division and not to seek after it. But teach me also to stand up for those things that I believe to be right, no matter what the consequences may be.*

*And help me this day to do some work of peace for You, perhaps to one whom I had thought to be my enemy.*

# 20

# BORN TO ETERNAL LIFE

*It is in dying that we are born to eternal life.*
—Prayer of St. Francis

What did St. Francis mean by this? Was he speaking of the afterlife, the life after death? The story of his dying relates that he had no fear of death. There was not a thought in his mind that his death meant the end of his relationship with his friend and his Most High Lord. On the contrary, it would continue, and it would continue forever. Yet it was not in this dying that he entered into eternal life; he had done that already, in his first dying, which began when he came down from his horse that day on the Umbrian plain.

It seems to me that in his prayer, St. Francis is speaking of the first kind of dying. When we give, something is given to us. When we pardon, pardon is given to us. So when we die, life is given to us. St. Francis is not speaking of some event not yet come. He is speaking of an event of which he has already had experience, of an event that is continually, perhaps continuously, happening. He is speaking of the kind of life of which Jesus spoke when He said that He had come so that we might have life and *"have it more abundantly"* (John 10:10). In other words, He had come so that we might have eternal life.

This view seems confirmed by the last stanza of "The Canticle of the Sun," which he added a few days before his death:

> Praised be my Lord for our sister, the bodily death,
> From which no living man can flee.
> Woe to them who die in mortal sin,
> Blessed those who shall find themselves in Thy most holy will,
> For the second death shall do them no ill.

It is difficult for many Christians to wholly adopt this interpretation of eternal life because they are preoccupied with what is called the afterlife, the life after death. The view is often held by Christians that if there is no life after death, then life before death has no meaning. This life after death has been described both by those who have had no experience of it, and (so we are told) by those who are actually experiencing it, according to whom it appears to be one of great insipidity. The descriptions of those who have no experience of it are, inevitably so, more imaginative. There seems to be a great deal of singing and praise and music in heaven, according to some. According to others, we take up where we left off. According to yet others, we are reunited with loved ones; this is the comfort given by many priests and ministers to bereaved persons. One of the latest and most imaginative efforts was made very recently by an English Swedenborgian who—in defiance of Jesus's statement that there is no marriage in heaven—asserts that those who have bad marital luck on earth will have good (and new) marital luck in heaven.

I should like to set down here my own belief. In so far as I am willing to be made an instrument of God's peace, in that far have I already entered into eternal life. Heaven to me is here, and whatever else it may be, I can know it now in so far as I am the instrument of that peace. What happens to me after I die, I do not know, nor do I really want to know. I have no evidence on which to deny that there is life after death, but what kind of life it would be, I have no idea. That a man who, in the words of Francis, was in God's will remains in that will, I am prepared to believe, because Francis, when death came, welcomed it; he called it "Sister Death" and said to his doctor, "She is to me the gate of life." So should I like to die.

There are some diffident Christians who cannot believe that they are now in eternal life, not only because they continue to think of eternal life as a reward for this one, but because they think it is far too grand a way to describe the prosaic way in which they live. They feel that such descriptions must be reserved for the saints and perhaps the clergy! Yet the gospel is a gospel for *us*; it is good news for *us*. When Jesus said, *"You are the light of the world"* (Matthew 5:14), He was not speaking to the saints and the clergy; He was speaking to people like *us*. So let us think and reflect more on the proposition that we are even now in eternal life, and whatever happens after the physical death, we do so continue, for we are in God's will, and God's will continues.

Two last points: The dying of the first death is not always a dramatic encounter; sometimes it takes a long time. The second point is that we do not cease to be sinners because we enter into eternal life; both St. Paul and St. Francis claimed to be superlative sinners.

In her biography, *Saint Francis of Assisi,*[7] Elizabeth Goudge writes that in midsummer of the year 1224, Francis was carried back to Assisi to die. His pains were great and continuous. He was lodged in the Bishop's house, and an armed guard was set about it, in case the people of Perugia would try to take him to their own town.

At first the doctor evaded his questions, but Francis said to him, "I am not a cuckoo to be afraid of death. By the grace of the Holy Spirit I am so intimately united to God that I am equally content to live or die." When the doctor replied that he would die at the end of September or the beginning of October, Francis stretched out his hands and cried aloud with joy, "Welcome, Sister Death." ... He sent for Angelo and Leo and asked them to sing for him his *Canticle of the Sun,* and after they had sung it he added the stanza "Praised be my Lord for our sister, the bodily death."

From that day to the end there was always singing in his room, in which he joined when he was able. Elias, who was now Minister-General of the Order, did not think this seemly, and he asked Francis to stop it, but for once Francis disobeyed him, declaring that he was rejoicing in the Lord.

When he was near death, the brothers gathered round him asking for his blessing, Elias on his left, and Bernard, his first disciple, on his right. But Francis wished to bless Elias with his right hand, to show him that he knew he was penitent and wished to forgive him. Therefore he crossed his arms so that his right hand was on the head of Elias, and the crossed arms are now the symbol of the Franciscan Order.

7. Elizabeth Goudge, *Saint Francis of Assisi* (London: Gerald Duckworth & Co., Ltd., 1959).

Francis now begged to go home to the Portiuncula, and how could Elias now deny him? Though he was blind he knew when the road reached a point where there was a clear view of Assisi. He asked to be placed facing it, and raising himself and his hand also, blessed the city and its people.

Home at the Portiuncula, he made a strange request. He asked to be well clothed upon his bier, and to have candles about him, and a cushion for his head. He saw no sin in it, because his body would be dead and would feel no pleasure. He dictated a last letter to Lady Clare, beseeching her in no wise to depart from the holy life and from poverty.

He asked his brothers to remove his tunic and lay him naked on the ground. There he lay with his left hand covering the wound in his side. Seeing him thus lie, the Father Guardian of the Portiuncula brought his own tunic and breeches to cover him, and to forestall Francis' refusal he said to him, "I lend you this tunic and breeches, and in order that you may know you have no right of property in them, I deprive you of all power to give them to anyone else." Francis' face lit up with joy, and for two reasons, for this speech was meant to acknowledge that Francis had always been true to his vows of poverty, but it was tender and teasing also, a remembrance of the many times that Francis, to the despair of the brothers, had given away all that he possessed.

When they put him back on his bed, he was content though in much pain. The next morning he asked for his brothers, and for a loaf of bread to be broken in pieces, and he gave to each of them. This was their last meal together.

When he was about to die, he asked again to be laid on the ground, and with what voice was left to him, he sang the 142nd Psalm, beginning, "I cried unto the Lord with my voice; with my voice unto the Lord did I make my supplications," and ending, "Bring my soul out of prison, that I may praise thy name; the righteous shall compass me about, for thou shalt deal bountifully with me."

And having so sung, he died.

Some people say that the days of faith are over, that Francis of Assisi lived in times that will never be known again, and that is why he was able to die singing. Such people should read that glorious book *Dying We Live*,[8] which contains the last letters of German men and women, some of them very young, who accepted death under Hitler rather than *lose their integrity*, as George N. Shuster says. What do those words mean—*lose their integrity*? Mr. Shuster seems to suggest that it is something one keeps even though one is dead. And this is a proper thought about a book called by the title *Dying We Live*.

This book is so full of courage, faith, and compassion for those who will be bereaved—and gratitude and surprise that God should have selected such weak instruments—that one could quote it forever. I shall quote only one thing. On February 18, 1943, Hans Scholl, age twenty-three, and his sister Sophie, age twenty-one, were caught dropping copies of the leaflet *Pamphlet of the White Rose* from a gallery into the main lobby of the University of Munich. One wonders at such courage in 1943, at the time when the Russians were turning the tide of war. One of this group was Christoph Probst, age twenty-three. He was sentenced to death on February 21, and along with the Scholls, he was executed on February 22. His mother and sister were allowed to read his farewell letters in the presence of the Gestapo but were not allowed to keep them. This is how they remembered Christoph's letters:

8. Helmut Gollwitzer, Käthe Kuhn, and Reinhold Schneider, ed., *Dying We Live: The Final Messages and Records of the Resistance* (New York: Pantheon Books, 1956).

- *To his mother*: I thank you for having given me life. When I really think it through, it has all been a single road to God. Do not grieve that I must now skip the last part of it. Soon I shall be closer to you than before. In the meantime I'll prepare a glorious reception for you all.
- *To his sister*: I never knew that dying is so easy. ... I die without any feeling of hatred. ... Never forget that life is nothing but a growing in love and a preparation for eternity.

**Welsh poet Henry Vaughan**: O my most blessed and glorious Creator, thou hast fed me all my life long, and redeemed me from all evil: seeing it is Thy merciful pleasure to take me out of this frail body, and to wipe away all tears from mine eyes, and all sorrows from my heart, I do with all humility and willingness consent and submit myself wholly unto Thy sacred will. My most loving Redeemer, into Thy saving and everlasting arms I commend my spirit: I am ready, my dear Lord, and earnestly expect and long for Thy good pleasure. Come quickly and receive the soul of Thy servant which trusteth Thee.

## *PRAYER*

*Lord, give me grace to die in Thy will. Prepare me for whatever place or condition awaits me. Let me die true to those things I believe to be true. And suffer me not through any fear of death to fall from Thee.*

*Lord, give me grace to live in Thy will also. Help me to master any fear, any desire, that prevents me from living in Thy will. Make me, O Lord, the instrument of Thy peace, that I may know eternal life.*

*Into Thy hands, I commend my spirit.*

21

# YOU WERE BOUGHT FOR A PRICE

*Everyone should live the life that the Lord gave him and to which God called him. This is my rule in all the churches. Was anyone circumcised when he was called? He should not try to change that. Was anyone uncircumcised when he was called? He should not get circumcised. Circumcision is nothing, and uncircumcision is nothing, but obeying God's commandments is everything. Everyone should stay in the same condition in which he was called. Were you a slave when you were called? Do not let that bother you. Of course, if you have a chance to become free, take advantage of the opportunity. For the slave who has been called to belong to the Lord is the Lord's free person. In the same way, the free person who has been called is the Messiah's slave. You were bought for a price. Stop becoming slaves of people.*

—1 Corinthians 7:17–23 (ISV)

When St. Paul writes of slavery and freedom, he is writing of institutions of his own times. But he is also playing on the words, and what he has to say has a meaning not dependent on time or place. He is saying that the man who is a slave of Christ is free, and the man who is free in Christ is a slave.

It is hard to comprehend this twofold paradox, yet we often comprehend it readily enough in other spheres. When we hear great music, we say that we are spellbound. When we hear a great speech, we say that the speaker *holds us*—and perhaps we add, "in the palm of his hand." A great actress enthralls us, literally holds us in thrall. A book grips us. A song captivates us. I think it was the Americans who introduced to the English language the expression "I am sold" (presumably into some kind of captivity).

One common element in all these bondages is the experience of being free. It is in being bound that we are free—not only free, but free in some exciting way.

Another common element is the element of love. We say we love music if it binds us and makes us free. We say we love the theater if it enthralls us and makes us free. We say we love a game if it fascinates us and makes us free. The music, the play, or the book may make us weep, may fill us with that indescribable mixture of pain and joy, but what makes us weep and dance and laugh is not just the music or the play or the book, it is something that rises in us: we are glad to be what we are; we have been caught up into that bondage that is perfect freedom.

When I was a young man, my student days over, I was influenced for a while by an unwilling belief in a rigid determinism, that choice and will were illusory, that we are what we are because of all the external forces that made us: our parents, friends, school, society, world, our physiology, and our metabolism, and all the rest of them. I lived in a race-caste society, and I was determined to get out of it, although it was physically more comfortable to live in it, to identify with it, even to be ready to die for it. What force was working there inside me? Was it simply another product of parents, friends, school, society, world, physiology, metabolism? Yes, in a way it was. But today, I believe that was nothing more than an out-view, one which saw myself as a tool, a toy, a thing to be moved about by forces external to myself. Today I do not understand these external forces; today I hold an in-view, one which sees myself as a self, made no doubt by many forces beyond my control, but gaining in coherence and integrity as I grow older. I am no longer a determinist; I am, in so far as a man can be, a self-determinator. That is one of the freedoms that the gospel gives to us: a belief in our worth as persons, a belief in what we can *do* as persons, a belief in what we can *be*. And no one helped me more to understand it than Francis of Assisi.

Why did Jesus hold those who listened to Him spellbound? It was because He showed them they were not helpless victims in the grip of fears, hates, the past, the world. They were the salt of the earth, the light of the world. He showed them a new thing—that obedience and freedom are inseparable. For where is the joy of living in a society in which all obey, and none is free? Or in which all are free, and none obeys? Something in them rose up to meet Him; they were caught up into the bondage that is the perfect freedom; they became His servants and His freedmen; they became His followers and His disciples. In Him, they found meaning for their lives, and there is no freedom like the freedom of finding meaning for one's life, of becoming the instrument of a Lord who helps us to be what we were meant to be. Yet many resist Him, believing that to follow Him is to lose the whole world.

It was granted to a sinner, not to a saint, to say this in unforgettable words.

**Francis Thompson, "The Hound of Heaven"**

I fled Him, down the nights and down the days;
  I fled Him, down the arches of the years;
I fled Him, down the labyrinthine ways
  Of my own mind; and in the mist of tears
I hid from Him, and under running laughter.
Up vistaed hopes I sped;
And shot, precipitated,
Adown titanic glooms and chasmed fears,
  From those strong Feet that followed, followed after.
But with unhurrying chase,
And unperturbed pace,
Deliberate speed, majestic instancy,
They beat—and a Voice beat
More instant than the Feet—
"All things betray thee, who betrayest Me."
I pleaded, outlaw-wise,
By many a hearted casement, curtained red,
  Trellised with intertwining charities;
(For though I knew His love who followed,
Yet was I sore adread
Lest, having Him, I must have naught beside)
But, if one little casement parted wide,
  The gust of His approach would clash it to.
  Fear wist not to evade, as Love wist to pursue. ...

And that is the heart of it—"Yet was I sore adread, lest, having Him, I must have naught beside." This was also the dread of St. Augustine—"*Give me chastity and continency, but do not give it yet*"—the dread that was overcome by the grace of God when Francis of Assisi came down from his horse and kissed the leper on the Umbrian plain.

## *THE PRISON HOUSE*

I ran from the prison house but they captured me,
And he waited me at the door with a face of doom,
And motioned me to go to his private room,
And he took my rank from me and gave me the hell
Of his tongue, and ordered me to the runaway cell
With the walls and the chains and the long night-days and the gloom.

And once on leave that goes to the well-behaved
I rose in fright from the very brothel bed
And through the midnight streets like a mad thing fled
Sobbing with tears lest the door be closed on me,
But nothing he did to me, he let me be,
No word but your clothing's disarranged he said.

And once in a place where I was, a man did ask
Whence I was, and he said, I never thought to see
A man from that place, and I wish I could be
In that place, by God I wish that I could be there,
I wish I was there, and I went back on air
And he met me there at the door, and he smiled at me.

And once when he took the whip to my rebel flesh
With foul and magnificent words I cursed and reviled

His name and his house and his works, and drunken and wild
I took the whip from his hands and slashed him again
And again and again, so he paid the price for my pain,
Till I fell at his feet and wept on the stone like a child.

He can take the hide from my back, and the sight from my eyes,
The lust of my loins, and the comforts of memory,
Fruit's taste, and the scent of the flowers, the salt of the sea,
The sounds of the world, and the words of magic and fire
That comforted me, so long as he does not require
The chains that now are become like garments to me.

## *PRAYER*

*Lord, we give thanks for the life and works of Thy servant and freedman Francis of Assisi, and for the help and hope that knowledge of his life has given to us and to countless others.*

*Lord, make us also the instruments of Thy peace.*

# ABOUT THE AUTHOR

Alan Paton (1903–1988) was a man of God and an internationally best-selling author whose now all-time classic debut novel, *Cry, the Beloved Country* (1948) is reported to have sold over 15 million copies. Twice adapted for film as well as a Broadway musical, it has been translated into numerous languages around the world.

Paton began his career as a teacher and later director of a boys' reformatory, where he introduced what were then considered to be controversial reforms, with the intention of bringing dignity and freedom to the troubled urban African boys in his care.

He later toured correctional facilities across Europe, Britian, and North America, and it was during this journey that he first began writing *Cry, the Beloved Country.* Paton secured a publisher with the help of his new American friends. His editor was Maxwell Perkins, who worked on the novels of Ernest Hemingway and Thomas Wolfe.

Back in South Africa, Paton found himself in the newly established apartheid regime, where policies of extreme racial segregation were being introduced. In response, Paton and others formed the Liberal Party of South Africa to counter apartheid. At one point, he went into hiding with his wife Dorrie.

In 1960, Paton traveled to New York to receive Freedom House's annual Freedom Award. Upon his return to South Africa, authorities confiscated his passport for a decade, making it impossible for him to leave the country. Paton's political party, comprised of both black and white members, was ultimately forced to dissolve in the 1960s.

In addition to his critically acclaimed novels, Paton also wrote numerous books of nonfiction, including two memoirs, poetry, plays, and short stories. He is noted for his psalmic and balanced prose style.

*Instrument of Peace,* formerly titled *Instrument of Thy Peace,* has a special place in Paton's oeuvre. Written while his wife Dorrie lay dying, Paton refused to give in to the despair he undoubtedly felt at the time. Instead, he encourages us to remember the prayer of St. Francis of Assisi:

*O Divine Master, grant that I may not so much seek to be consoled, as to console; not so much to be understood, as to understand; not so much to be loved, as to love.*

# Welcome to Our House!

*We Have a Special Gift for You*

It is our privilege and pleasure to share in your love of Christian books. We are committed to bringing you authors and books that feed, challenge, and enrich your faith.

To show our appreciation, we invite you to sign up to receive a specially selected **Reader Appreciation Gift**, with our compliments. Just go to the Web address at the bottom of this page.

God bless you as you seek a deeper walk with Him!

WE HAVE A GIFT FOR YOU. VISIT:

whpub.me/nonfictionthx

WHITAKER HOUSE